100 Questions (and Answers) About Survey Research

Q&A SAGE 100 Questions and Answers Series

Visit **sagepub.com/100qa** for a current listing of titles in this series.

100 Questions (and Answers) About Survey Research

Erin Ruel

Georgia State University

Los Angeles | London | New Delhi
Singapore | Washington DC | Melbourne

FOR INFORMATION:

SAGE Publications, Inc.
2455 Teller Road
Thousand Oaks, California 91320
E-mail: order@sagepub.com

SAGE Publications Ltd.
1 Oliver's Yard
55 City Road
London EC1Y 1SP
United Kingdom

SAGE Publications India Pvt. Ltd.
B 1/I 1 Mohan Cooperative
Industrial Area
Mathura Road, New Delhi 110 044
India

SAGE Publications Asia-Pacific Pte. Ltd.
3 Church Street
#10-04 Samsung Hub
Singapore 049483

Printed in the United States of America

Library of Congress Cataloging-in-Publication Data

Names: Ruel, Erin E., author.

Title: 100 questions (and answers) about survey research / Erin Ruel, Georgia State University.

Other titles: A hundred questions (and answers) about survey research

Description: First Edition. | Thousand Oaks : SAGE Publications, [2018] | Includes bibliographical references and index.

Identifiers: LCCN 2018034664 | ISBN 9781506348827 (pbk. : alk. paper)

Subjects: LCSH: Social surveys—Methodology. | Scientific surveys—Methodology.

Classification: LCC HM538 .R84 2018 | DDC 300.72/3—dc23
LC record available at https://lccn.loc.gov/2018034664

This book is printed on acid-free paper.

Acquisitions Editor: Helen Salmon
Editorial Assistant: Megan O'Heffernan
Production Editor: Jyothi Sriram
Copy Editor: Diane DiMura
Typesetter: Hurix Digital
Proofreader: Tricia Currie-Knight
Indexer: Robie Grant
Cover Designer: Candice Harman
Marketing Manager: Susannah Goldes

MIX
Paper from
responsible sources
FSC® C008955
www.fsc.org

18 19 20 21 22 23 10 9 8 7 6 5 4 3 2

Contents

Preface

Surveys are ubiquitous. Every day, people are asked to take surveys, from research studies, marketing programs, to politics, and polling. If we are receiving a barrage of requests to participate in surveys, then there are many people and organizations out there creating those surveys. Using survey methodology may seem easy, and certainly many of the tools, such as SurveyMonkey, may make it seem even easier. However, a well-conducted survey is actually quite complicated and difficult to achieve. There are many hard-to-see pitfalls that can harm a survey study and invalidate the survey results. If we are being asked to take so many surveys, wouldn't it be nice to know we aren't wasting our time on a poorly designed survey? Understanding survey research methods, then, is incredibly important.

100 Questions (and Answers) About Survey Research will walk the reader through the survey process from beginning to end: from developing a research question, designing the right survey, writing survey questions, cleaning and analyzing data, and finally writing it up.

100 Questions (and Answers) About Survey Research can be used in the classroom as a supplemental book for a research methods or survey course in a variety of social science disciplines. Graduate students working on theses or dissertations may find its comprehensiveness useful. It can also be used by the new or seasoned practitioner as a resource or guide to conducting a well-designed study from start to finish.

The questions are divided into 10 parts as follows:

- Part 1: Understanding What Surveys Are and How They Are Used

- Part 2: Addressing Ethical Concerns in Survey Research

- Part 3: Selecting a Sample

- Part 4: Writing Good Survey Questions

- Part 5: Establishing the Reliability and Validity of Survey Questions

- Part 6: Conducting the Survey

- Part 7: Entering and Cleaning the Data

- Part 8: Exploring the Data With Univariate Statistical Analysis

- Part 9: Assessing Associations With Bivariate Statistical Tests and Regression

- Part 10: Writing Up the Analyses in Report Form

This book is designed to flow from the start of a survey research project to the end of the project. Therefore, it can be read cover to cover. But the set-up lends itself well to focusing on specific topics or questions as issues arise while conducting a survey. Given that research is iterative and non-linear, jumping around from question to question may work well for some.

This book is not comprehensive. It touches on important topics such as validity and reliability. But there are whole books written just on validity and reliability. Psychometrics and the field of education have developed these topics beyond the scope of this book. We encourage you to further your knowledge by seeking out more information on these topics.

Statistics is a field unto itself, too. Again, statistics are introduced and discussed because a survey is useless if we cannot correctly analyze the data we have collected. Many of the basics of statistical analysis are included, but the reader is encouraged to consult a statistical text as well.

Each question ends with a reference to three other related questions—possibly with additional questions occasionally referenced in the text of the answer. While each question and answer is independent, all the topics of surveys are interrelated. These are the three questions we think can best supplement the primary question and answer, but of course, other questions can supplement as well.

Acknowledgments

I would like to acknowledge and thank Neil Salkind for starting this series, and Helen Salmon and the editorial staff at SAGE. Also, I would like to thank the following reviewers for their time and careful critique of this manuscript:

Nicholas Clark, Susquehanna University

Melinda Jackson, San Jose State University

Jenni L. Redifer, Western Kentucky University

James Wright, University of Central Florida

Michael TenEyck, University of Cincinnati

Luke Duesbery, San Diego State University

Anthony J. Santella, Hofstra University

Derrick M. Bryan, Morehouse College

John M. Kennedy, Indiana University

Nicole C. Ralston, University of Portland

Shane Day, Portland State University

Preston B. Cosgrove, Cardinal Stritch University

Carie Green, University of Alaska Fairbanks

About the Author

Erin Ruel is Professor of Sociology at Georgia State University. She teaches research methods at the undergraduate and graduate levels. Her research interests are in stratification, inequality, neighborhoods, housing, and health disparities. She has engaged in survey research on stratification and aging, housing and health, community land trusts, and environmental justice. She has published over thirty peer reviewed articles and book chapters. She is also co-author of the book, *The Practice of Survey Research* (SAGE, 2015).

Understanding What Surveys Are and How They Are Used

What Is a Survey?

A survey is a tool used to collect data on a large group of people to answer one or more research questions. It is one of the most common research tools used by social science research (sociology, political science, education, and psychology), health fields, and market research. And frankly, every corporation these days that wants feedback on a service or product surveys their customers. Surveys are that versatile and interdisciplinary.

When we think of a survey, we are thinking of the survey instrument: a questionnaire used to collect information on a large group of people. While the survey instrument is extremely important, it is only one aspect of the entire survey design process. To conduct a high-quality survey, we also need to carefully plan the correct survey design (e.g., single point in time, multiple time points) to answer the question. How we will administer the survey needs to be carefully considered. Additionally, we will need to determine how we will collect, contact, and convince our survey respondents to participate in the survey.

Lastly, we need to prepare ahead of time for how to analyze the resulting survey data. The answers to the survey questions are the data we analyze. Each survey question becomes a variable (what we analyze in the data) in the resultant data. All data need some level of preparation prior to analysis. Some survey studies will require "data entry," which simply means entering the data into some sort of statistical software package. Most survey data collections will need "cleaning" and creation of variables.

At every step of the process, we need to remember that we are undertaking a survey in order to answer empirical research questions. "Empirical" means a real-world question—a question that can be answered with facts. This should drive all aspects of the survey research design.

More questions? See questions 2, 3, and 4.

How Are Surveys Used?

S urveys are used for a broad array of purposes. The American government uses surveys for basic research, as well as for evaluating policies and programs. The Study of Income and Program Participation is a government-funded survey study designed to examine how well federal income support programs are operating. Survey questions from this study include information on housing subsidies, food subsidies, and income supports. The U.S. census is a federally funded study that uses the survey format to count the entire population every 10 years. It's not a true survey study because it uses the full population rather than a sample. Resources are allocated to the 50 states based on the results of this study.

Social scientists use surveys for basic or applied research. The General Social Survey is a survey administered every 2 years or so that focuses on attitudes and opinions of the American people. Researchers use this data regularly to determine how attitudes are changing over time and what might explain those changes. Researchers also use surveys to answer specific research questions, such as who voted in a given election or who they voted for. This would be a basic research question in that the results do not have a specific immediate use, whereas an applied research question would be designed with a specific outcome in mind. For example, a survey to answer the question *What are the needs of homeless and runaway youth in Atlanta?* would be used specifically by organizations whose goal it is to help homeless youth.

Corporations use surveys to find out how satisfied customers are with their services or products and what companies might do to improve performance going forward. Nonprofits may use surveys to determine if their programs are working well, or if and how they could be improved. Anyone can use a survey for answering an empirical question.

More questions? See questions 3, 4, and 6.

3

What Are the Benefits of Doing a Survey?

S urveys have several great properties that make them ideal to answer almost any type of research question. Surveys are versatile, cost effective, and generalizable.

Surveys are versatile in that any research topic or question can be made to work well as a survey. Many disciplines in the social sciences use survey data, such as sociology, political science, psychology, education, health sciences, social work, and many more. In fact, about a third of all academic publications use survey data, attesting to its popularity.

There are repositories of publically available survey data that anyone can use (most is available at www.ICPSR.umich.edu). While some questions may not fit your concepts as well as you would like, you can still answer a research question easily and inexpensively by using publically available survey data. Many social scientists make a whole career out of analyzing secondary use, publically available survey data and never create their own surveys.

Surveys are efficient in terms of time and resources because, relative to the number of questions that can be asked and the number of people that can be surveyed, the value of the results far outweighs the costs of administration. To be clear, survey research is not inexpensive in terms of either money or time commitment. Researchers can spend enormous amounts of time planning a study, implementing a study, cleaning and analyzing the data, and finally in writing up the results. However, surveys, once designed, are relatively inexpensive. That is, adding an additional question or additional participant does not increase the cost very much.

The last major strength or benefit of surveys is generalizability, which means that the information found in the survey is representative or reflective of the entire population being studied—not just the sample collected. Not all surveys take advantage of this strength of the survey method, meaning that simply doing a survey does not mean that the results are generalizable. In order for us to be able to generalize, we must rigorously follow the proper sampling techniques (coming in Part 4).

More questions? See questions 1, 2, and 4.

QUESTION

4

What Is the Survey Research Process From Beginning to End?

The process starts by having a question that we want to answer using a survey. We focus first on making sure it is the best possible version of the research question. We do this by reading existing research on the same topic first to see if someone has already answered the question, but secondly, to see what the existing research questions look like. Based on the reading of prior research, we may decide to edit or even change our initial research question.

Question

design

Once we have a research question, we can choose the best survey design to answer that question. We then figure out who are the best people to conduct the research on. This has two purposes. First, it helps us decide the best way to administer the survey. For example, if we are interested in young adults, perhaps an online survey makes the most sense. The second purpose is to figure out how to collect a sample. As part of this decision, we need to know how large a sample to collect to have the ability to answer our research question.

The next step is to create the actual survey instrument by coming up with well-measured survey questions that will collect the right information to be able to answer our research question. In addition, we will want to think about how to organize the survey instrument or questionnaire. How do we want it to look to attract participation? What is the best question ordering? Once these are accomplished, we reach out to our sample with recruitment material, and convince them to participate and take the survey. The final steps in the process are to enter the data from the completed surveys. Then we clean the data, analyze the data, and write up the final report. The report should detail the survey research process and provide the answer to the research question. Each of these steps is laid out in the remaining chapters of this book.

More questions? See questions 5, 6, and 7.

6

QUESTION

5

How Are Good Empirical Research Questions Developed?

S ince the research design is driven by the research question, it follows that we want to have the best possible research question. A research question is one that can be answered by collecting empirical observations, such as answers to a survey, which can be analyzed. The results of the analysis will answer the research question. A question that focuses on beliefs or ideologies often cannot be answered using social science methods because we cannot collect observations about things that are not empirical, meaning observations about the real world. While we can ask if people agree with a particular ideology like neoliberalism, for example, or if they believe in God, we cannot prove that God exists using survey research.

Exploratory questions are also not good questions for survey research. Exploratory questions ask about meanings, rituals, experiences. We often want to get at these things in people's own words and definitions. Qualitative research is better for this type of research, as surveys are designed to collect shallower information on a lot of people—not deep information on a few people. This is one disadvantage of the survey.

A good research question is one that has been carefully thought out and precisely stated. If it is too general or vague, the correct data might not be collected, and therefore, we won't do a good job of answering the research question. An example of a vague research question is *How do people get ahead in life?* It is vague because we don't know what is meant by getting "ahead." Do we mean becoming rich, or do we mean something else? The question also seems to assume that people will get ahead in life, that getting ahead is everyone's goal. But there are different pathways or goals. When doing research, we need to think through these assumptions and determine if they are valid and OK for our research.

We continue revising the research question until the concepts we wish to analyze are concrete and observable. We may change "getting ahead in life" to "buying a home." Lastly, we want to evaluate if our research question is socially and scientifically relevant. If we expend a lot of resources to conduct a survey, we want to make sure we are studying something important.

More questions? See questions 4, 6, and 7.

What Are the Various Types of Survey Design?

The most typical survey design is the cross-sectional design. Researchers, using a cross-sectional design, survey people at a single point in time. This is adequate to answer most research questions. In Question (Q) 5, we ended with home buying. The research question could be, *At what age do people buy a home?* Or *Who doesn't buy a home?* These are examples of research questions that can be answered with a cross-sectional design.

However, if we are interested in change over time, we would select a longitudinal design. There are two types of longitudinal designs. The first is a panel design in which the same people are surveyed multiple times. The second is a time series or trend design. In this design, a different group of participants is selected at each time point. For this design, we

Table 6.1   Survey Design Types and Their Properties

	Cross-Sectional	Panel	Trend/Series
Type of Design	Survey one group at one point in time	Survey several points in time, same people each time	Survey several points in time, different people each time
Benefits	Inexpensive Describe what's happening at a single point in time	Can see individual level change	Can describe trends in opinions over time Can test for population level change
Costs or Constraints	Hard to get people to participate	Expensive Hard to get people to participate People may decide to stop participating	Expensive and hard to get people to participate

could examine age of home buying for different periods of time, as this gives us multiple cross-sectional snapshots over time. For a panel design, we might change "getting ahead in life" to "acquisition of wealth." We could ask *Are Americans able to save enough (wealth accumulation) to be able to retire by age 65?*

Table 6.1 lists the three survey design types along with their costs and benefits. A major benefit of cross-sectional design is that it is relatively inexpensive. With a cross-sectional design, we can gather a good snapshot of social life at one point in time. With a panel design, we can get a dynamic view of social life. We can see individual change over time. A trend design gives multiple snapshots of social life. We can see change occurring at the level of the nation, but not within people. In terms of costs, all three struggle with the difficulty of getting people to agree to participate. Panel studies also suffer from attrition, which is people stopping their participation partway through the study.

More questions? See questions 4, 5, and 7.

How Do We Choose the Right Survey Design?

We choose the research design based on the research question we intend to answer. There are three broad categories of research questions used: (1) descriptive, (2) explanatory, and (3) evaluative.

Descriptive questions are ones that ask how much of X is out there. For example, we might ask, *What is the prevalence of diabetes in the United States in 2018?* This question is asking for a snapshot of 2018; therefore, a cross-sectional design would work well. If, however, we asked *How has the prevalence of diabetes in the United States changed between 1990 and 2018?*, we are asking for a whole bunch of snapshots. In this case, a trend study would be the best design.

Explanatory questions are those that ask about the relationships between two or more variables. For example, we might ask, *Does obesity cause diabetes?* Or, *Does living in disadvantaged neighborhoods increase the probability of a diabetes diagnosis?* The first question is asking about causation: *Does increased weight cause diabetes?* Causation is best answered with a panel design so we can see change over time within participants' weight and diabetes diagnoses. The latter question can be answered with a cross-sectional study. In a cross-sectional design, the data will tell us about the differences in diabetes diagnoses for those living in varying neighborhoods.

Evaluative questions are a special form of explanatory question that are used specifically to evaluate (causally) social programs or interventions. These questions ask, *Is this program effective?* Or, *Will a program of exercise, combined with nutrition, lower the risks of diabetes?* Generally, some form of panel design is best for this type of question. A before-and-after program design would be ideal.

More questions? See questions 4, 5, and 6.

Addressing Ethical Concerns in Survey Research

What Are the Main Ethical Concerns of Research?

R esearch ethics are primarily concerned with three aspects of research, as found in Table 8.1: (1) the research participants themselves, (2) the data collected from the participants, and (3) how we present our findings.

Table 8.1 Areas of Ethical Concern for Researchers	
Ethics Area	**Ethics Issues**
Research Subjects	Do no harm, informed consent, minimizing risks, maximizing benefits
Data	Clear documentation, transparency, and replicability
Presenting Findings	Responsible interpretations of the data, sticking close to the data

Most ethical issues in research come from medical research, in which people can be physically harmed by participating. However, all researchers are expected to do no harm to human subjects. Or, if there is potential harm, we need to minimize the harm and maximize the benefits of conducting the research. In surveys, there are few immediate benefits for participating, but there are also few risks.

Researchers should also carefully document all the procedures followed for collecting the data, creating the dataset out of the surveys, and analyzing the data. A clear protocol for making decisions when data are not very good should be followed consistently, and these decisions should be transparent and available to anyone who asks for them. High levels of transparency and documentation are tedious but necessary for others to be able to replicate findings. Replication means that other researchers can duplicate our methods and findings—an important aspect of scientific progress.

Researchers have an obligation when presenting findings to do so in a way that masks the identities of the research participants. Researchers also need to be sensitive in how we portray findings. Valid interpretations need to be easy for all to understand. We researchers have an obligation to see that our findings do not harm anyone, especially not vulnerable or marginalized groups of people.

More questions? See questions 9, 13, and 14.

9

If Surveys Are Just About Asking People Questions, Why Are Ethical Considerations Important?

How we approach research can have ethical implications. Oftentimes, we think we know the answer to the research question, but we want to confirm it with evidence. Believe it or not, our personal beliefs and assumptions can influence the research design in such a way that the results will reflect our expectations. That is, we can accidentally bias our own research. In fact, even the research questions we ask can expose our biases. For example, research comparing the IQs of Whites and Blacks makes the implicit assumption that there are important biological differences to be found. Researchers need to be open to the possibility of being wrong. Ethically, as researchers, we need to be able to separate out our personal agendas from our research agendas. Having to think ethically about our personal agendas and our expectations can improve the study design.

Conducting social science research is a privilege and an important responsibility. It is very possible that a survey, despite merely asking questions, can be harmful. Asking women questions about sexual abuse or rape might lead to serious emotional harm. We need to have some structure set in place to help participants who do experience grave emotional harm. For example, a resource guide might be put together to assist any participants who experience distress. Other participants might be very vulnerable, such as children or institutionalized people such as prisoners who may feel pressured to participate. It is not ethical to take advantage of the vulnerable.

If research findings lead to policy changes, but the findings are wrong, then participants, as well as other people, may be harmed. Science itself and people's trust in science and facts may also be harmed. Once policy is made, it is very difficult to change it. Therefore, we researchers, ethically, must do everything in our power to ensure the soundness of the research question, the research design, the analysis, and presentation of the study results. We need to be transparent in our methodological documentation and make it publically available. This will ensure the best possible outcome despite any flaws that may arise.

More questions? See questions 8, 15, and 16.

Who Ensures That Research Is Ethical?

There was no ethical oversight of medical research until after WWII, when the atrocities of the Nazi's research agenda were made public. In the United States, research ethics violations continued through to the 1970s, however. For example, the 40-year-long Tuskegee study, examining syphilis in Black men, continued long after a cure was found, but without providing the men with the cure. In 1974, the National Research Act established the Institutional Review Board (IRB) system for regulating research with human beings, which exists today.

All universities that engage in federally funded research have their own IRB that oversees that university's human subject's research. An IRB is a committee, made up of university members and local community members, whose purpose is to oversee all aspects of a university's research involving human subjects, including approving the research design, monitoring data collection, and protecting the rights of participants.

In 1991, 16 federal government agencies adopted the core of these 1974 regulations in a common policy to protect human subjects known as the Common Rule. The "core" is espoused in the 1978 Belmont Report's focus on (1) beneficence, (2) justice, and (3) respect for persons. All university IRBs are empowered by regulations from the Food and Drug Administration and the Office for Human Research Protections of the Department of Health and Human Services to oversee that university's research.

Funding agencies will not disperse research funding until a research project has been awarded IRB approval. For that matter, research projects cannot be started until IRB approval has been received. University researchers also receive regular training in conducting human-subjects research. This too is under the purview of the IRB.

More questions? See questions 8, 11, and 12.

11

How Do IRBs Monitor Research Ethics?

Research projects involving human subjects must be submitted to a university's IRB for approval prior to engaging in the collection of data. The submission will include all aspects of the research design, as well as specific information for dealing with human subjects. This will include a statement of the risks and benefits to the potential participants, what groups of humans will be included in the study and why, how the privacy of the human subjects will be maintained, and how the participants will be informed about the study.

The 1978 Belmont Report cites three core values as important for human subjects research: beneficence, justice, and respect for persons. "Beneficence" means to minimize harms and maximize benefits. This will be included in the IRB statement. "Justice" means that all groups of humans are equally likely to be included unless there is a good research reason not to. This also will be included in the IRB statement. "Respect for persons," the last value, is captured by the informed consent form. Participants have the right to be fully informed about the research and decide for themselves whether or not to participate. This is accomplished with an informed consent form. This is how participants learn about the study and how their privacy will be maintained.

IRB contact information is included on informed consent forms so that participants may contact them if they have a complaint. This is another way for IRBs to monitor research. When this happens, research investigators will submit an adverse event form to the IRB. If there are too many adverse events, the IRB may shut the research down. Each year, ongoing research projects must receive continuing review. Research should stop until continuing review is approved.

There have been cases of research projects violating IRB protocols. When this happens, the federal government has been known to step in and shut down all research at a university for six or more months until the issue is resolved. This is extremely harmful to a university and is a strong motivating factor in researchers complying with IRBs.

More questions? See questions 10, 12, and 13.

What Is the Process of Submitting a Survey Study to the IRB?

Each university's webpage will have links to its IRB. This is important because each university's IRB will operate differently. The university IRB webpage will have instructions on how to submit to the IRB, as well as examples. The process usually starts with attending human subjects training and becoming certified to work with human subjects. This is often done through CITI training, which is a group that specializes in training university faculty and students on medical or social and behavioral ethics of working with human subjects. Please google "CITI training" for more information.

Once we are certified to conduct research with human subjects, we submit our research study to the IRB. Again, there should be a written process on how to do it specifically on each university's webpage. For conducting a survey, we will need the following things to submit a study: (1) a research methodology; (2) an informed consent form; (3) specific language on how we will keep participants' confidential identities or anonymous; (4) recruitment material or scripts we plan to use to convince people to participate; (5) any incentives we plan to use to thank participants for completing the research; and (6) a human subjects statement on the risks and benefits of the study, a description/justification of the study population, and a statement if we are using vulnerable populations or special populations rather than the general population.

The IRB application process includes a lot of questions and justifications for many aspects of the research decisions made. One decision is whether the proposal will need a full board review, be expedited, or be exempt. The full review (by all members of the IRB) takes place if the human subjects are vulnerable to some degree or if there is risk of harm to human subjects. If there is no more risk of harm than in a normal day to subjects, the research protocol can go through expedited review. "Expedited" means just a couple members of the IRB will assess the submission. "Exempt review" means the research does not involve identifying participants in any way. Generally, only an IRB can classify the research as exempt. It is often helpful to meet with an IRB member for advice prior to submitting.

More questions? See questions 11, 13, and 14.

13

What Is Informed Consent?

In research, informed consent is the process whereby researchers explain the research study to prospective participants, and hope they will agree to undertake the study. It general, it is a form that includes information on what the survey study is, any risks or benefits to participants, any possible incentives, and how participants' privacy will be maintained. Only with this knowledge can participants make an informed decision about whether or not to consent to participate. Researchers need to be honest and transparent with their research subjects in terms of explaining to participants all that is involved in the research study.

Informed consent is most often obtained through participants signing the informed consent form. There are times when waiving a signature might be beneficial, such as when a signature might be the only documentation that a person participated in the survey. If anonymity is the desired form of privacy for participants, then signed consent forms could violate that. In this type of case, consent can be verbal, and an informed consent statement can be given to the participant for his or her records. For example, in a 2015 survey of homeless and runaway youth in Atlanta, we obtained a waiver of signed consent in order to ensure anonymous participation.

If conducting research on children, consent can be more difficult to obtain. If the children are old enough to read, understand the study, and consent to participate, researchers will need both the child participant and a parent to consent. If the children are very young, they may not be able to read yet or sign a form. Researchers will have to read the consent to the children and ask questions to determine if the child participants understand consent.

This raises an important point about consent. IRBs like to have consent forms written at a ninth-grade reading level. The United States has a diverse citizenry and not all go to college or even finish high school. A ninth-grade reading level will make the form understandable to the majority of citizens. In fact, all recruitment material and the survey itself should be written at the ninth-grade reading level to ensure comprehension by the majority.

More questions? See questions 11, 12, and 14.

QUESTION

14

What Are Confidentiality and Anonymity, and How Are They Maintained?

Confidentiality and anonymity are two possible ways that researchers can maintain the privacy of research participants. Anonymity is when participants' names are not linked in any way to the survey data. Perhaps a unique number is created to be used on each survey to indicate a person, but even the researchers do not know which person that number represents. Anonymity is possible only with cross-sectional designs.

But if we want to keep track of who has participated and who still needs to participate, confidentiality may be the better option. "Confidentiality" means that the researchers may be able to link participants to the survey data, but no one else can. And the link does not exist within the data, but only in some separate spreadsheet or list that only the researcher can see.

With longitudinal panel designs, confidentiality is the best way to achieve privacy. We will want to link each person's data from one survey to the next. Researchers will need to keep track of participants over time and so will need a list of names and contact information. Participants can be matched from one survey to the next using that unique number. In other words, the same unique identifiers will be used for the same participants from one survey to the next.

When reporting findings, we want to continue to keep identities private or confidential. Instead of presenting individual-level information such as female, African American, mid-thirties, professional tennis player (one of the Williams sisters?) that can risk a participant being identified, researchers should only present grouped or aggregate findings. Fifteen percent of the sample are African American, and 1% are professional athletes. In this way, no one can figure out the identity and data of any one participant. Since we are not interested in individuals, but societal issues and relationships between concepts and ideas, focusing on grouped data should not be a hardship.

More questions? See questions 12, 13, and 15.

15

What Are the Ethical Concerns for Collecting and Analyzing Data?

So far, we have focused on ethical treatment of research subjects. While rare, some researchers have been known to cheat when it comes to conducting research. This is known as falsifying or fabricating their data. This is also unethical and covered by the IRB.

Fabrication is the literal making up of data. Rather than collecting data, a researcher might just create a dataset. In 2015, *Science,* a highly regarded academic journal, retracted a paper about canvassing people regarding their attitudes toward gay marriage. Researchers attempting to replicate the study found many irregularities. When they delved further into the study to understand why they could not replicate it, they found that the company that was supposed to have collected the data had not. The primary researcher was unable to produce the survey data. This is highly unethical and likely to ruin the researcher's career permanently.

There can be more dire consequences, however. A 1998 study falsely linked autism to the MMR vaccine (measles, mumps, and rubella), causing parents to stop vaccinating their children. This led to an increase in measles among children, and for some, death from measles.

Falsification involves changing the data or suppressing data or results that do not fit with theoretical expectations. It is also defined as the intentional distortion of data or findings. It also may include misrepresenting the findings or the methods or both in a publication. Falsification differs from fabrication in that the data are real, collected from real participants, but for some reason, are not considered good enough. Falsification can take the form of making the data appear to be more valid and reliable than they really are. Some researchers may publish only the results that fit with their research agenda.

Fabrication and falsification are pretty serious. There could be times when falsification is due to simple negligence, rather than willfully misleading the scientific community. One way to ensure no falsification is to write up every data decision, variable creation method, and analysis type as transparently as possible. Making these write-ups publically available will protect a researcher from accusations of falsification. An IRB will not catch fabrication or falsification unless they are tipped off to it. Therefore, researchers must vigilantly monitor their own research actions.

More questions? See questions 8, 9, and 11.

Selecting A Sample

PART 3

Who Is Asked to Take the Survey?

One important aspect of the survey research project involves defining the population, or entire set of people, on which we want to conduct research. In other words, we define who the population is for each study. There are two reasons for this. First, this is the group that is pertinent to answering our research question. Second, this is the population to whom we will generalize our results. Generalization (see Q3), is a key goal of research and means our findings on the sample will apply to the whole population.

The Americans Changing Lives Study (ACL) defines their population for its survey as American adults age 24 or older living in the 48 contiguous states (not including Alaska or Hawaii) who live in typical households, but not in group quarters. Group quarters are defined as institutional living such as jails, nursing homes, hospitals or halfway houses. This is a detailed population definition.

Once the population is carefully defined, we determine if we have the resources to take a sample from that population. Oftentimes, researchers will "target" one aspect of the population for the sake of feasibility. For example, a researcher in the Midwest might define the population as all voting-age adults living in America. She may then target voting-age adults in the Midwest, as access to them will be easier and cheaper. By targeting a feasible portion of the population, the researcher has changed who the sample represents. Now the sample only represents voting-age Americans living in the Midwest. It is important to remember and write down these decisions so that later, when we are interpreting our findings, we do not generalize to the wrong population.

More questions? See questions 3, 4, and 17.

What Is a Sample, and What Is Sampling?

A sample is a subset of the population of individuals needed to answer a research question. We collect only a sample of the population because it is often too expensive and difficult to collect survey data on the entire population (a census). The population itself will change before we would be able to complete our study—some will die, some will migrate in or out, and others will be born. This suggests that collecting a subset of the population may, in fact, be better than collecting the whole population for answering most research questions.

Sampling is the process of collecting a sample from the population. Sampling techniques fall into two broad categories: (1) probability sampling techniques and (2) nonprobability sampling techniques. A probability sampling method is one that allows chance alone to dictate who is selected into the sample. It allows us to know the probability of a person being selected into the sample as well as the probability of an entire sample being selected. A nonprobability sampling method is one in which the probability of selection into the sample is unknown. There are a variety of sampling methods that fall within these two broad categories.

In general, we want to use a probability sampling technique because only with a probability sampling method can we ensure that our sample represents the population from which it came. In order to calculate the probability of selection, we need to know the size of the population and list them in some way. We do this with a sampling frame, or list of the population. It is not always possible to create a sampling frame. There are modifications such as stratified or cluster probability sampling techniques that can help with that problem (see Q26–Q28). When it is impossible to create a sampling frame even with modifications, we are limited to nonprobability sampling and therefore cannot generalize to the population.

More questions? See questions 16, 18, and 20.

What Is a Sampling Frame?

D rawing a probability sample starts by enumerating all members of the population. We call this list of all population members a sampling frame. It is necessary for collecting a probability sample. If we cannot create a sampling frame, we will have to either modify our sampling technique or switch to a nonprobability sample (introduced in Q17). If we were collecting a sample of U.S. states, our sampling frame would consist of the full population of U.S. states, of which there are 50. Knowing the population size allows us to calculate the probability of being selected into the sample (see Q20).

It is important to make the sampling frame as accurate as possible. U.S. states are easy to enumerate, but we are usually interested in people, and lists of people are less easy to find. If we use a phone book to find people, we will miss those people without a phone and those who refuse to be listed in the phone book. This creates a type of sampling error called coverage error. If a particular group of people are less likely to be included on the sampling frame, then our sample will not be representative of members of that group. This means our sample findings will be biased (inaccurate) rather than representative of the population.

Oftentimes we use several lists of people to create our sampling frame. This improves coverage because people not on one list may be on another list. This introduces a new problem of some people being on the sampling frame more than once. This will increase their probability of being selected into the sample compared to those listed only once. This too will bias the sample. Unlike random sampling error, bias is a problem. Therefore, we need to devote considerable time and resources to creating the best possible sampling frame.

More questions? See questions 17, 19, and 23.

How Do We Know if the Sample Size Is Large Enough?

This question is asking how large of a sample is needed in order to answer the research question with statistical significance. If a true relationship exists in the population, but our sample size is too small, then the association between our two concepts (effect size) will not be statistically significant. We will falsely reject that there is a relationship between them. We call this the "power" to detect an effect.

There are several online freeware applications that can help us determine the correct sample size. Before we can use them, however, we need to know some terms that go into the power analysis equation. We need to know "Alpha," "Beta," and the "effect size," or size of the relationship between our two variables of interest. The Alpha (α) criterion represents the risk of falsely rejecting a relationship when there is one. It is generally set at .05. The reverse problem, finding a relationship in the sample when none exists in the population, is known as Beta (β). Power to detect an effect is defined as $1-\beta$, or the probability of finding an effect in the sample when it is true in the population. Lastly, we have to know what the effect

Table 19.1   Cohen's Sample Size Table

Beta	Power ($1-\beta$)	Cohen's d (Effect Size)		
		.2 (small)	.5 (medium)	.8 (large)
		n	n	n
.25	.75	84	14	6
.5	.5	193	32	13
.8	.2	393	64	26
.9	.1	526	85	34
.99	.01	920	148	58

Source: Cohen, Jacob. (1992). "Statistical Power Analysis." *Current Directions in Psychological Science, 1*(3), 98–101.

size might be. This is difficult especially if no one has researched this yet. If there is previous research, we can see what the effect size was and whether it was a positive or negative effect in other studies. If not, we can do a pilot study—a preliminary, smaller study on the same population—and use the findings to determine the effect size.

Because determining effect sizes is so difficult, one statistician created a table of potential sample sizes for a range of power levels and for small, medium, and large effect sizes (Cohen, 1992). It is presented in Table 19.1. As we can see in Table 19.1, when Beta is small, we have plenty of power to detect an effect. Therefore, the sample sizes are much smaller when Beta is .25 than when it is .90. Sample sizes can also be smaller when the effect size is larger. For example, in the row with Beta = .50, if the effect size is small, then we need a sample of 193 to detect a relationship between our two variables. If the effect size is medium or large, to detect that effect, we need samples sizes n = 32 and 13 respectively. In general, a sample of size 200 ought to be large enough to capture most effects.

More questions? See questions 17, 20, and 21.

How Does
Probability Work?

G enerally speaking, probability theory, sampling theory, and a statistical theorem called the Central Limit Theorem explain how a probability sample can represent the population. We will start with probability theory.

If we flip a coin, what is the probability tails will appear rather than heads? There is a 50% probability or *chance* that tails will appear. How did we get that? There are two sides to a coin, so the denominator for this event is 2. There is one event, tails, so the numerator is 1. We divide 1 by 2 and get .50 or 50%. Probability, then, measures the likelihood that one event will occur out of all possible outcomes. Probability ranges between 0 and 1 with 0 meaning the event absolutely will not occur, 1 meaning the event absolutely will occur, and .50 meaning it is as likely to occur as not occur.

What if we wanted to know the probability of drawing an ace from a pack of cards? Well, we need to know how many cards are in a deck for the denominator: 52. We need to know how many aces are in a deck for the numerator: four. We divide 4 by 52 and get .0769. The probability of selecting an ace is quite low at 7.7%. This is a rare event.

Returning to sampling, to know the probability of selecting a sample (event), we need to know the size of the population for the denominator (sampling frame) and the size of the sample we want to collect for the numerator. So, if we collect a sample of 10 cards from a deck of 52, the probability of any sample of size 10 would be 10/52 = .19, which is the same as selecting one card at a time (1/52) * 10 = .019 * 10 = .19. This assumes that once the card is selected, we do not place it back into the deck. That is generally a good assumption for a sample. We do not want to select one person to be in our sample multiple times. So, we almost always sample without replacement.

More questions? See questions 17, 21, and 22.

What Is Sampling Theory?

W e are interested in characteristics about the population, like income, for example. We don't know the average income of the population, however. So, when we collect a sample of the population and take the mean (average) income of the sample, we do not know how well it reflects the population mean income.

Let's say we draw a sample of size n, take the mean income from the sample, and toss it back. Then choose another random sample of size n, take the mean of income, and toss it back. Sampling theory tells us that if we do this an infinite number of times, and plot all the sample mean incomes, we would eventually get a bell shaped distribution (see Figure 21.1) with the centermost point being the mean income level of all the infinite number of samples drawn ($\overline{Y}$). The mean of the sampling distribution also turns out to be the mean of the population mean ($\acute{u}$).

The bell curve has great known characteristics that help us understand how well the sample can generalize to the population. Fifty percent of all sample means will be on either side of the mean. Furthermore, 68% of all samples will be within one standard deviation (measure of dispersion about the mean) of that population mean, and 95% will be within two standard deviations, leaving 2.5% of samples in each tail.

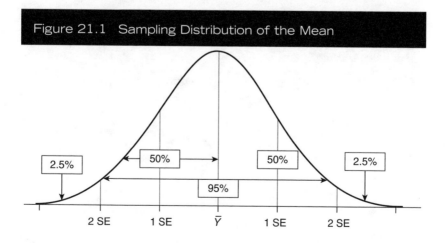

Figure 21.1 Sampling Distribution of the Mean

2.5%   50%   50%   2.5%

95%

2 SE   1 SE $\overline{Y}$ 1 SE   2 SE

Now if it isn't feasible to survey the entire population, it certainly isn't feasible to survey an infinite number of samples. However, 95 times out of 100, the one random sample we can afford to collect will be within two standard deviation of the population mean. This tells us that the mean income in the sample will closely resemble the population mean income for most samples. In other words, sampling theory tells us that the mean of the sampling distribution is an unbiased estimator of the population mean.

More questions? See questions 17, 18, and 22.

What Is the Central Limit Theorem?

The Central Limit Theorem states that as the sample size *n* approaches infinity, the mean of the sampling distribution (presented in Q21) approaches the normal bell-shaped distribution. This theorem is telling us that the size of the sample is very important. The larger the sample size, the better the sampling distribution will be and the more closely the sample mean for some variable will reflect the population mean for that variable. In other words, the larger the sample size, the narrower the bell curve will be, and the smaller the sample size, the wider the bell curve will be.

The general rule of thumb is that we need a sample of at least size n = 200 to ensure that the sampling distribution of the mean will approach a bell-shaped distribution. Also, if the population is very diverse or heterogeneous, then a larger sample is necessary compared to when the population is very homogenous or not very diverse. This increases the probability of including all the diversity in the sample.

If our population is very large, then a sample of 200 will probably not be adequate. The Americans Changing Lives Study (ACL) is a nationally representative sample with a sample size of 3,617 individuals. The National Survey of Families and Households (NSFH) is a nationally representative sample of 13,007 households. Both are representative samples because both used probability methods to collect the sample, but one is much larger than the other. What does this mean? The bell curve distribution for NSFH ought to be narrower than that of ACL. This in turn means that the standard deviation—or variability about the mean— will be much smaller for NSFH compared to ACL. Finally, it means that both produce unbiased estimates of the population mean, but that the NSFH sample will most likely produce less random sampling error (difference between sample mean and population mean) than will the ACL sample.

More questions? See questions 20, 21, and 23.

What Is Random Sampling Error?

As mentioned in Q22, random sampling error is the difference between the population mean and sample mean of some variable. A sample collected using a random sampling method from a known population distribution will be representative of the population, but it will not exactly replicate the population. In fact, if we drew two independent and random samples of 1,000 college students and averaged their GPAs, the average GPA from each sample would likely not be the same. Nor would either sample exactly match the population mean GPA level.

In Table 23.1, we calculate the sampling error as the population mean less the sample mean. Sample 1 and Sample 2 have sampling error or variability in opposite directions and of different size or magnitude. If we took an infinite number of independent samples and averaged all the mean GPAs together, the mean of the sampling distribution would be 3.25 or the population mean.

All samples have some random sampling error. Statistical techniques can handle random sampling error. Still, we want to minimize sampling error. Because we are collecting only one sample, we know it will deviate from the population mean on any given variable, but we usually do not know the population mean and therefore cannot determine exactly how much error exists.

Table 23.1 Sampling Error Example

	GPA	Sampling Error
Sample 1	3.54	−.29 (3.25 − 3.54)
Sample 2	3.08	.17 (3.25 − 3.08)
Population	3.25	

More questions? See questions 20, 21, and 22.

What Are the Types of Probability Samples?

There are three main types of probability samples: (1) simple random sampling, (2) stratified sampling, and (3) cluster sampling. But there are variations on each type plus ways to combine them. Therefore, there are a large number of ways to sample. Sampling can become extremely complicated fast. This book will cover the three basic forms. Going beyond these basic forms often requires the consultation of a statistician even for expert surveyors.

A simple random sample is one in which each person in the population is listed on a sampling frame. A number is assigned to each person. Then, using a random number generator, a sample of size n is collected. In this type of sampling, each person has an equal and positive chance or probability of being selected into the sample.

A stratified random sample is a variation on the simple random sample that guarantees that the distribution of the sample will exactly reflect the population on whatever characteristic is used to stratify. For example, in a study of racial health disparities among adults in Atlanta, Georgia, we would want to ensure representation of all races. Atlanta is diverse in terms of most racial groups: Whites, African Americans, Asians, and Hispanics; however, there are very few Native Americans. A simple random sample may end up with no Native Americans in the sample. Therefore, we would choose to conduct a stratified random sample where we stratify the sampling frame by race (this assumes we have racial information included in the sampling frame) to ensure representation. Every person has a nonzero probability of selection, but it is not the same.

A cluster sample is used when we cannot create a sampling frame of the population of interest, but we can for some organization in which our population is clustered. For example, there is no way to get a listing of third graders. We can get a list of all schools that include third grade, however. So, we create a sampling frame of the population of elementary schools, and then take a simple random sample of schools. Then we survey all third graders in each school cluster. Third graders in selected schools have a 100% probability of selection; others have a zero probability of selection.

More questions? See questions 20, 25, and 26.

How Is a Simple Random Sample Collected?

L et's return to our sampling frame of 50 states. Let's say we want a sample of size 10 ($n = 10$) states. How do we collect it? Well, we could put the name of each state on a slip of paper, stick the 50 slips of paper into a bag, mix them up, reach in, and blindly select 10 slips of paper. This is called random sampling without replacement because we pulled all 10 slips of paper at the same time. If all 10 states are pulled at the same time, the probability of being selected is a function of the sample size divided by the population size, n/N or $10/50 = 1/5$ or .20. This probability sample is called a simple random sample. The probability of selection is the same for all samples. It is the best sampling method to use.

With 50 states, pulling slips of paper from a bag is easy and not too time consuming. If we are selecting 1,000 people from a population of 2 million, then this is not going to work. Again, we create our sampling frame of people and assign a number to each person. Next, we can go online and use a free random number generator program to pull a sample of 1,000 numbers without replacement. Each random number is completely independent of all other numbers, which means using a random number generator is as random as pulling slips of paper from a bag. We then find the person associated with each selected number and add him or her to our sample list. The probability of selection of any random sample of size 1,000 without replacement is n/N or $1,000/2,000,000 = .00050$. This is the more standard way to collect a sample for a survey.

It is random because chance is the only thing predicting which person gets selected into the sample. Each possible sample has the same probability of being selected. Each person also has an equal probability of being selected into the sample.

More questions? See questions 17, 18, and 23.

What Is Stratified Random Sampling?

A stratified random sample is a variation on the simple random sample that guarantees that the distribution of the sample will exactly reflect the population on whatever characteristic is used to stratify it. There are two types of stratified random samples: proportionate stratified sampling and disproportionate stratified sampling. A proportionate stratified sample selects a sample that has the same distribution as the population on the stratifying variable (i.e., race). If stratifying on race, the racial distribution of the sample will exactly match the racial distribution in the population.

A disproportionate stratified sample, on the other hand, purposefully does not match the population distribution on the stratifying variable. One reason to use a disproportionate sample is to ensure all groups, even really small groups, are included in the sample in large enough numbers that we can conduct statistical analyses that include them. For example, in Atlanta, Asians make up just over 5% of the population. This may mean there will be too few Asians in the sample to understand the needs of Atlanta's Asian residents. Therefore, we will want to ensure that Asians disproportionately make up 15% of the sample.

When we use a disproportionate sampling method, our sample no longer reflects the population, and so we cannot generalize back to the population. We can correct for this by creating sample weights. The sample weight is simply the inverse of the probability of selection for each stratum or group, or $1/n_i/N_i$ where i stands for each stratum. That is, a different weight will be calculated for each stratum. We will discuss sample weights in detail in Q29.

With stratified sampling, the probability of being selected into the sample will vary across each racial group. This introduces more than just chance as the selector of the sample. The sample may precisely represent the population in terms of the stratifying variable, but may not represent the population well in terms of other variables we are interested in. Therefore, when we deviate from the simple random sample, we may increase error.

More questions? See questions 27, 28, and 29.

QUESTION

27

How Is a Proportionate Stratified Probability Sample Collected?

We start by creating sampling frames like we would for a simple random sample. In this case, we create a separate sampling frame for each category of the stratifying variable. If race is the stratifying variable and there are five racial categories, we will have five separate sampling frames. Then we will collect a simple random sample from each sampling frame. If the ultimate sample size we want is $n = 1,000$, then we determine how much of that total sample size should come from each racial group. Table 27.1 provides the necessary information to calculate that and the probability of selection for each stratum.

Since Whites make up 38% of the population, we want to ensure that 38% of the total sample size of 1,000 come from the White stratum. So we multiply 1,000 by 38% and we get an n of 380 Whites for the sample. We repeat this step for each racial group and find that our sample will include 540 African Americans, 50 Hispanics, 30 Asians, and two Native Americans. The sample racial distribution is now exactly the same as the population racial distribution.

The probability of being selected into the sample is calculated as the sample size for each stratum divided by the population size of each stratum. For Whites then, it would be 380/175,105 or .0022. As you can see from the last row of Table 27.1, in a proportionate stratified sampling, the probability of selection into the sample is the same for each racial stratum. We use a number generator again to select each stratum's sample (see Q25).

	White	African American	Hispanic	Asian	Native American	Size
Population	38% N = 175,105	54% N = 246,241	5% N = 22,800	3% N = 13,680	0.2% N = 912	456,002
Proportionate	38% n = 380	54% n = 540	5% n = 50	3% n = 30	0.2% n = 2	1,000
Probability of Selection	0.0022	0.0022	0.0022	0.0022	0.0022	

Table 27.1 Example of Proportionate Stratified Sampling

More questions? See questions 25, 26, and 28.

28

How Is a Disproportionate Stratified Probability Sample Collected?

Again we start by creating a sampling frame for each category of the stratifying variable. Using the same example as in Q27, we stratify on race and will collect five simple random samples from each stratum. We want a total sample size of $n = 1,000$. We start by specifying how many individuals we want to include in our sample from each racial stratum. In this case (see Table 28.1), we have specified that we want 100 Hispanics, Asians, and Native Americans in the sample and 350 each of Whites and African Americans. Next we determine the racial distribution of the sample by dividing $n/1,000$ (total sample size) for each stratum. We can see that for Native Americans, we are obtaining 10% sample distribution, which is much larger than the .2% population distribution (oversampled). To calculate the probability of selection, we divide the desired sample size $n = 350$ for African Americans by the population size, $N = 246,241 = .0014$.

In this sample, some of the racial strata are overrepresented, meaning we obtain more than their proportionate size in the population, and other racial strata are undersampled, meaning less than their proportionate share is selected. In Table 28.1, we can see that African Americans are undersampled (35% versus 54%) while Hispanics, Asians,

Table 28.1 Example of Disproportionate Sampling

	White	African American	Hispanic	Asian	Native American	Size
Population	38% $N = 175,105$	54% $N = 246,241$	5% $N = 22,800$	3% $N = 13,680$	0.2% $N = 912$	456,002
Disproportionate	35% $n = 350$	35% $n = 350$	10% $n = 100$	10% $n = 100$	10% $n = 100$	1,000
Probability of selection	0.0020	0.0014	0.0044	0.007	0.11	

and Native Americans are oversampled. Notice that in disproportionate sampling each stratum has a different probability of selection into the sample. We use a number generator again to select each stratum's sample (see Q25).

More questions? See questions 25, 26, and 27.

How Do We Make Disproportionate Stratified Samples Representative of the Population?

In Q28 we noticed that in a disproportionate stratified sample, some strata are overrepresented and others are underrepresented so that it no longer represents the population. In order to make the sample generalizable, we can create weights in all the statistical analyses that will bring the sample back to representativeness.

What are weights? Weights are the inverse of the probability of selection. Weights tell us how many population strata members each sample member represents. The last row of Table 29.1 provides the weights for each stratum. To calculate the weight, we simply divide 1 by the probability of selection for each stratum. The weight for Native Americans is 1/.11 = 9. This means each Native American sample participant represents nine Native Americans in the population, whereas each African American in the sample represents 714 in the population. We can use these weights in statistical analyses on a disproportionate sample in order to bring the sample statistics back to representativeness.

Table 29.1 Example of Disproportionate Sampling

	White	African American	Hispanic	Asian	Native American	Size
Population	38% $N = 175,105$	54% $N = 246,241$	5% $N = 22,800$	3% $N = 13,680$	0.2% $N = 912$	456,002
Disproportionate	35% $n = 350$	35% $n = 350$	10% $n = 100$	10% $n = 100$	10% $n = 100$	1,000
Probability of Selection	0.0020	0.0014	0.0044	0.007	0.11	
Weight	500	714	227	143	9	

We are not changing the sample. Rather, in the statistical analyses, each participant is weighted by his or her stratum's weight (multiplied by the weight), which changes the statistical calculations to bring them in line with the population racial distribution.

More questions? See questions 26, 27, and 28.

30

How Is a Cluster Sample Collected?

Cluster sampling is useful when our population cannot be listed on a sampling frame, but is clustered or organized under some grouping that *can* be listed on a sampling frame. For example, third graders cannot be listed on a sampling frame, but elementary schools can. We can use elementary schools as clusters of third graders.

Let's say we are interested in the math development of third graders. We can randomly select a probability sample of schools. We do not yet have our sample of third graders, however. Once we have the schools, we can request a listing of all third-grade students in each school. One option would be to take all third graders in each selected school. If we have a random sample of 10 schools and eight of them have 200 third graders and two of them have 90 third graders, we will have a sample of 1,780 third graders in only 10 schools. This may not be feasible in terms of costs, however, as some schools may be very large. Therefore, we may decide to take a random sample of third graders from within each selected school.

In general then, cluster sampling takes two stages: (1) sampling of the clusters (schools); and (2) sampling of people within the selected clusters (third graders). At each stage, a simple random or a stratified sample can be collected.

The second option, choosing a sample within clusters, has the added benefit of increasing diversity in the sample. Schools tend to be homogenous, meaning that kids who go to the same school tend to have a lot in common. Across schools, however, kids may be very different. Therefore, if we collect more schools (clusters) and fewer third graders within each cluster, we maximize variation while maintaining feasibility. In other words, we can collect a sample of 1,800 third graders by randomly selecting 600 schools and then randomly selecting 30 third graders from each school.

Our first example gave us a sample of 1,780 from 10 schools, and the second example gave us 1,800 from 600 schools. The two-stage sampling process decreased within school homogeneity and increased diversity and representativeness. The probability of selection is more complicated. It is a combination of the probability of a school being selected multiplied by the probability of a child within a given school being selected. So, all third graders will not have an equal chance or probability of being selected into the sample. This might introduce some sampling error.

More questions? See questions 23, 24, and 25.

31

How Do We Select a Sample if the Population Is Not Easy to Find?

Selecting a random sample is based on being able to locate and list all population members on a sampling frame. The population is not always available for us to list. Some populations, such as the homeless or the marginalized (drug users, drug dealers), are not easy to find. They are not listed in phone books and they don't advertise their occupations and hobbies or have clubs or associations. Therefore, a random sample is not always possible.

When we cannot create a sampling frame, we have to use a nonprobability sampling method. Nonprobability samples are not generalizable. So, turning to a nonprobability sample means losing one of the greatest strengths of survey research, so do all that you can to get a probability sample prior to resorting to nonprobability samples.

There are four main types of nonprobability sampling techniques. The first is called a convenience sample: literally, finding those people who are convenient to survey. The mall surveyor is a great example of someone asking shoppers at the mall to take a survey. The people who shop at that particular mall may not at all represent the full population. The second type is a quota sample. A quota sample is a convenience sample that builds variability into the sample by having quotas. Market research is the best example of this. Market researchers will conduct a survey and make sure that half the participants are male and half are female. Once all females are collected, they will not survey anymore females and will focus on collecting the males. The third type is a judgment sample, or a purposive sample. This is a type of convenience sample where the researcher is interested in a particular type of knowledge. The average person will not have that knowledge. If interested in hiring procedures, hiring personnel at big corporations will be the best informers. We will select all hiring personnel conveniently based on willingness to talk to us. The last type is a snowball sampling method or respondent-driven sampling. This is a chain referral method used with hard-to-find populations like the homeless. We find one or more homeless people and ask them to introduce us to more homeless people. Then we interview those homeless and ask them to introduce us to more homeless, and our sample grows in this way like a snowball.

More questions? See questions 16, 17, and 18.

What Is a Response Rate?

O nce we select the sample of persons we want to survey, we need to approach them and ask them to take the survey. Not everyone will agree to participate in the survey study. In fact, it is getting harder and harder to get people to agree to participate. This is problematic because the sample is representative at the size selected, but it may not remain representative if too many people refuse to participate. We determine this by calculating a response rate.

The response rate is the percentage of the selected sample that completes the survey or the ratio of those who agreed to participate divided by the sample size. For example, if a sample of size $n = 1,000$ is selected, and 500 agree to participate, then the response rate is 500/1,000 or 50%.

If some of the sample members are ineligible, meaning they do not fit the population criteria, or they died, then the sample size (denominator) can be reduced to exclude them. For example, if the sample again is $n = 1,000$, and 500 agree to participate, but 100 did not participate because they didn't fit the population criteria, then the response rate is 500 / (1,000–100) or 500/900 = 55.6%.

Generally, a sample is still considered representative if it has a minimum response rate of 70%. Therefore, researchers strive to get at least 70% of the sample to agree to participate. This means that 30% did not participate, which is known as the nonresponse rate. It is often helpful to determine if the nonrespondents, or people who refused to take the survey, are different in any way from those who did take the survey. For example, if those who refused to take the survey are less likely to graduate high school compared to those who do take the survey, then the study is not representative of the whole population, but only of those with high levels of education. This means that even if a study achieves a 70% response rate, it is possible that the final sample size of 700 rather than the 1,000 selected will not be representative of the population.

More questions? See questions 17, 20, and 21.

Writing Good Survey Questions

33

What Is Involved in Writing Good Survey Questions?

W riting good survey questions is one of the most important tasks of the survey process. Each survey question is attempting to measure an important theoretical construct that is derived from the theory and research question that we are exploring. The responses to the survey questions are our observations. These observations or responses to all the survey questions are turned into data and analyzed to answer the research question that started this process.

In addition to the above requirements, all the questions in surveys are standardized. This means that the question wording never changes—it is the same for all study participants. Everyone answers the same question with the exact same wording. The implications of this is that all people, regardless of their background, their level of education, their nationality, or any of the other characteristics that make people unique, have to answer the survey question as it is written—with no modifications. In other words, conceivably someone with a seventh-grade education will have to answer the same question as someone with a Ph.D. Thus, questions must be written that both (all) types of respondents are capable of answering easily and accurately.

Most survey questions are also close ended, meaning the researchers provide a set of responses from which participants select the best answer. The set of responses need to work with the question, need to be exhaustive (a category for everyone), and need to be mutually exclusive (everyone fits in one and only one category).

The survey question needs to accurately and consistently capture the theoretic concept of interest. Reliability and validity are methodological terms used to evaluate whether a survey question is a good one. Reliability and validity will be explored in more depth in Part 5.

More questions? See questions 34, 35, and 38.

34

How Do We Connect a Theoretical Concept to a Survey Question?

A s stated in Q33, we want to answer a research question using observations to survey questions that we then analyze. Some concepts are simple, such as alcohol use, and others are more complex, such as family dynamics. The first step is to explore and understand exactly what is meant by each concept. To do this, we start by reading existing research on our concepts.

The existing literature on alcohol use might show that drinking is not as simple as we first thought. Alcohol use could be about regular use or about binge drinking. Furthermore, the level of use may depend upon age and gender. This process is called *conceptualizing*. If our sample consists of adolescents, then perhaps we are interested in any alcohol use, regular alcohol use, and episodes of binge drinking. That means we need to ask at least three alcohol use questions, one for each aspect of alcohol use we've conceptualized.

The next step is to write the actual survey questions that will capture the essence of what we want to know from each member of the sample. This process is known as operationalizing the concept. Each survey question can be thought of as an operation that collects observations or data on the sample. Each becomes a variable: ever drink, regular drink, and binge drink. We could ask

Q1. Have you ever had a drink (even a sip) of alcohol (beer, wine, or hard liquor)?

☐ Yes

☐ No

Q2. About how many alcoholic beverages do you drink in a typical week? ____(# of drinks)

Q3. Have you ever had 5 alcoholic beverages in a single evening (less than 5 hours)?

☐ Yes

☐ No

More questions? See questions 33, 35, and 36.

How Do We Write Survey Questions for Complex Theoretical Concepts?

As previously stated, sometimes a concept is simple and unproblematic. Recall that alcohol use was considered a simple concept, and yet, it could involve multiple survey questions to get at various aspects of the concept (see Q34). Some concepts are large and complex involving multiple dimensions. Some concepts are not observable in the empirical world and cannot be articulated easily, such as depression. It is only by asking multiple survey questions for each dimension of the complex concept that we begin to observe these complex concepts. Later, in the analysis stage, we can combine the answers to the series of survey questions into a single-scale variable (sum of several variables) that captures the complexity of the concept. For example, one depression scale variable (called the CESD) is made up of the responses to 20 separate survey questions.

Another example of a complex concept would be socioeconomic status. This concept seeks to understand people's locations in a hierarchy based on economic and social position. Some of the dimensions included in socioeconomic status are education, income, wealth, occupation, social class, and social capital. Some of these dimensions are easy to capture with questions. Others, such as social capital, are themselves complex concepts. One of our most important tasks is to conceptualize the concepts found in the research question in order to ensure the survey questions can be used to correctly answer the research question. Once this is accomplished, we can move on to the art and science of crafting survey questions.

More questions? See questions 33, 34, and 36.

36

Do We Need to Create New Questions, or Can We Use Existing Questions?

I f there are existing questions that have been shown to provide good results, it makes sense to use those existing questions. To know if existing questions will provide good results, we need to see the research that has used these existing questions and learn what the research on the existing questions says about their utility. It certainly speeds up the questionnaire design process if we can find existing questions. One place to search for existing questions is the Inter-university Consortium for Political and Social Research (ICPSR), a data archive at the University of Michigan (https://www.icpsr.umich.edu/index.html).

In checking on existing questions' validity and reliability, make sure to determine if they are culturally relevant to your population. Have the questions been used with multiple populations? Are they period sensitive, meaning valid a long time ago, but maybe not today?

One benefit of using existing questions is the ability to compare the results of your study to the prior studies that used the same questions. This is helpful also as a check to make sure our sample does reflect the population if both the prior study and our current study have samples from the same population. However, the same questions may not work on all populations. Therefore, if our population is different, we should stop and think about how it is different and whether or not the question will work with our population. Perhaps the questions will need some minor tweaking or a complete overhaul.

In order to determine the best question, we can use all the questions—existing and new ones—in a temporary questionnaire and then give the temporary survey questionnaire to a couple of experts in the substantive field and have them take the survey. Then we ask them which questions they thought worked the best in this pretest of the questionnaire. At this point, we can remove all the questions the experts think do not work.

More questions? See questions 34, 37, and 38.

What Are the Basic Rules to Writing Good Survey Questions?

Survey question writing involves both science and artistry. There are many sources that can be used to understand all the research on writing good questions. Here are some of the basic rules. People differ in terms of their levels of education, reading ability, and vocabulary. In order to have your questions be understood by the vast majority of people, keep the reading level of your questions to Grade 9 or lower. Use simple, clear, and precise language, and avoid abstract terms. This means use short questions with few clauses and use short words in your questions. Make sure one and only one question is included in each survey question. Definitions of some terminology may need to be included. Instructions should be detailed, easy to follow, and at a grade level that all can grasp.

Avoid negative question set-ups and especially double negatives because they are hard to understand and answer correctly. A negative set-up example is, *"Do you agree or disagree that most people are not happy?"* Why not ask, *"Do you agree or disagree that most people are happy?"* It is easier to answer, and those who think most people are unhappy will "disagree." An example of a double negative is *"In your opinion, should the Supreme Court not oppose women serving in combat positions in the U.S. military?"* This can be restated positively as *"Should the Supreme Court support or not support women serving in combat positions in the U.S. military?"*

This does not mean negative questions cannot be included, but make sure they are clear and easy to understand. For example, a question often included in depression studies is *"In the last 7 days, I have felt sad/blue/depressed."*

Finally, be consistent in your question set-up and instructions. This makes it easier for respondents to understand how to answer your questions. If it is a pen-and-paper survey, have them consistently circle the one correct answer—don't throw in the occasional check box, because that is confusing. If multiple answers rather than one correct answer are desired, give bolded instructions to ensure respondents understand.

More questions? See questions 33, 38, and 39.

38

Are There More Advanced Rules to Writing Survey Questions?

Yes, there are more advanced rules. First, avoid biased or leading language. Leading questions can use strong and biased words that are manipulative or mislead respondents to answer in ways desired by the researcher. This is just bad science that needs to be avoided. Unfortunately, this sometimes can happen unknowingly. To avoid this, have experts look over your questionnaire to seek out biased or leading language. Some words such as "approve," or other emotionally appealing language, when used in a question can create a bias known as social desirability. People are likely to provide the answer they think the researcher wants to hear. Other words may have special significance and if used could bias the response. For example, "welfare" has negative connotations and should be replaced with a more neutral term. The same should be done for words with overly positive connotations.

Concepts relating to behaviors, opinions, or attitudes that are more complex tend to yield less precise responses. Try not to use jargon-laden language for these; be straightforward, and use the present tense. Asking about the past can be tricky because we remember the past based on our present. Try to go only a short distance into the past. Ask about behavior in the prior month or possibly past 6 months. To go back any further risks incredibly imprecise responses. If we want to learn about behaviors or attitudes in the distant past, we will want to concretely remind the respondent of the past using an event history calendar that gives visual cues to help respondents place the past on a timeline.

Do not combine two separate questions into a single question with the word "and." These are called double-barreled questions. For example, *"Does abstinence only sex education work and do you approve of distributing condoms in high school?"* are two separate questions. A person might want to say yes to the first part and no to the second part. This is a very confusing question to include. Turn them into two separate questions.

More questions? See questions 33, 37, and 39.

What Are the Best Response Options to Use With Survey Questions?

Generally speaking, there are two types of response options, open and closed. Closed-ended questions are ones formatted to provide a list of responses from which the respondent chooses the answer. Open-ended questions are ones without response options that allow respondents to answer the question any way they want using their own words. In surveys, closed-ended questions are preferred because there is greater reliability across the respondents, there is greater anonymity for the respondents, data collection is quicker, and the responses are easier to quantify and analyze.

There are several types of closed-ended response categories researchers can choose. The multiple choice format is well known by most, as it is so often used on school exams. Racial categories (i.e., White, Black, Hispanic) are multiple choice. There can be dichotomous options (e.g., Yes/No). Response options can include a checklist in which respondents check off all that apply, such as a list of public services used in the previous month (e.g., library, DMV, food bank). There are several scale options available. The most common is the Likert scale, which is a 5-point scale of agreement ranging from "strongly agree" to "strongly disagree" with a neutral central value. One can also use a rank-order scale in which respondents rank order their preferences.

As with the questions, response categories should be clear, relevant, and unambiguous. They should also be exhaustive and mutually exclusive. "Exhaustive" means that every possible response option is available; it is comprehensive. Allowing a response of "Other" with a "please spec-ify_____" will make any set of responses exhaustive. "Mutually exclusive" means that a respondent will fit into one and only one response category. This means the categories should not overlap in anyway.

More questions? See questions 37, 38, and 40.

What Is the Measurement Level of a Survey Question, and Why Is That Important?

S ince we turn the responses to survey questions into variables to analyze to answer the research question, we must understand how the
variables we create are measured. Measurement, in essence, is replacing
text responses with numbers. Statistical analyses differ depending on the
measurement level of the variables. There are four levels of measurement:
(1) ratio, (2) interval, (3) ordinal, and (4) nominal. These four levels are
rank ordered in terms of ability to analyze the variables with ratio measurement being the most flexible, and therefore, the most desirable.

Ratio measurement is the most precisely measured mathemati-
cally. These are variables like age or income that have continuous values
ranging from zero, or lower in some cases, to infinity potentially. Ratio
variables have a true zero value, meaning that the zero makes substantive
sense. Someone born yesterday has an age of 0. This allows us to multiply,
divide, add, subtract, rank order, or group responses into categories. For
example, one person is twice as old as another, and 10 years older than
a third.

Interval measurement is very similar to ratio measurement, in that
variables have continuous values, but there isn't a true 0. Temperature is
a good example of an interval measurement. If temperature is measured
in degrees Fahrenheit, 32 degrees is considered freezing. In Celsius, 0 is
measured as exactly freezing. Temperature is a scale measurement with no
anchoring zero point, which means we can add or subtract, but not multiply or divide. The difference between 32 and 33 degrees Fahrenheit is not
the same as the difference between 0 and 1 degree Celsius.

"Ordinal measurement" means rank ordering. Likert scale items are
ordinal, meaning we know the order but we don't know the distances
between the categories. Therefore, we cannot even add or subtract. Nominal variables are qualitative or text variables, like Yes/No or racial categories
that cannot even be rank ordered. These are the most limited measure-
ments to work with. When creating survey questions, pay attention to
the measurement level and try for response categories that allow ratio and
interval measurement when at all possible.

More questions? See questions 37, 38, and 39.

When Are Open-Ended Questions Used in Survey Research?

G iven the strengths of closed-ended questions, why use open-ended questions in surveys? Open-ended questions are important in several situations: (1) when asking about a quantity, (2) following a closed-ended question to expand upon the closed-ended response, and (3) when the concept being observed is new and so potential responses are not yet known.

Open-ended questions may ask about quantities, such as "*How many miles do you drive to work on a given day?*" _____. Respondents are expected to fill in the blank with a number. This type of open-ended question is easy to code and use in quantitative analyses. This works well with dates, age, height, weight, income, and years of education, for example.

Open-ended questions provide more nuance, depth, and substance in their answers compared to closed-ended questions. However, they take more time for the respondent to answer and increase the burden we are placing on them. Additionally, the coding process needed to make open-ended questions useful in quantitative analyses with the other survey items is long and tedious. Furthermore, the final variables created in the coding process often lose the depth and nuance of the original answers. But a partial open-ended question, one with closed-response categories plus an "*Other, please specify response category*," will reduce the burden and allow for more variety of responses.

When creating open-ended survey questions that require text responses, try to ask questions that require long responses. That is, do not ask questions for which a yes or no will suffice. Save this type of question for when you truly do not know what answers you will get. In general, use open-ended questions sparingly.

More questions? See questions 33, 34, and 40.

How Do We Order the Survey Questions?

Think about the respondents when organizing the survey. What will be the least burdensome way we can put the survey together? For example, questions about similar subjects should be grouped together. Then, there can be instructions common for a group of questions rather than a different set of instructions for a single question. Questions with the same response options can be grouped together in a matrix form or table to make answering them easier.

Start the survey with instructions and remind the respondents that their identity will be kept confidential. Start with a question that will be of interest to your participants but also easy to answer. It should be directly related to your research question, and that will make them want to complete the study. However, it should not be a sensitive question. Put sensitive questions closer to the middle of the survey. Build up some rapport before addressing anything sensitive. In the instructions, we might want to remind participants that the survey is confidential when asking participants to answer sensitive questions.

The demographic questions should be the last section, unless demographics are at the heart of your study. If participants decide to stop before completing the survey, at least the most relevant questions will be answered. End the survey on a positive note. Leave the participants reflecting on something positive and happy, and hopefully that feeling will be associated with the survey. Don't leave the participants feeling down because the survey focused on poor health or inequality and ended with that. Instead, end with an open-ended question that asks about what positive improvements have happened recently to reduce inequality.

Finally, make sure the survey itself looks professional, has plenty of space between questions, and is consistent in the presentation of questions and response categories. It should be pleasing to the participants so that they will feel safe to take it.

More questions? See questions 2, 33, and 37.

Establishing the Reliability and Validity of Survey Questions

43

How Do We Ensure Our Survey Questions Measure What They Are Supposed To?

As noted in Part 4, we work hard to ensure our questions are clear and easy to understand. But how well do they measure the concepts we want them to measure, and do they measure them consistently? The terms we use to evaluate this are called "validity" and "reliability." By "validity" is meant accuracy—does the survey question accurately and precisely measure the concept of interest? Reliability gets at how consistently a survey question produces the same results if asked multiple times of the same participants.

Validity can be assessed in several ways, such as face validity, content validity, criterion-based validity, and construct validity. Face validity addresses whether or not, on its face, the survey question appears to measure the appropriate concept. This is not a particularly rigorous evaluation of the measurement of a survey question. Content validity is designed to determine if a measure (survey question) or series of measures captures all aspects or dimensions of a concept. Content validity has played an important role in developing measurement tests in the disciplines of education and psychology. Criterion and construct validity are more rigorous ways of assessing measurement validity and will be defined in later questions in this chapter. The issues of reliability and validity are really a concern about measurement error. If a survey question does not validly or reliably measure the concept of interest, then the concept is measured with error. The greater the measurement error, the less likely the survey question is to reflect the concept of interest and the less likely it is that the research question can be answered.

Measurement error is unavoidable, but we can try to minimize it. There are techniques such as pretesting, pilot testing, and cognitive interviews we can use (see Q50) to reduce measurement error and increase validity and reliability.

More questions? See questions 45, 46, and 47.

44

How Is Content Validity Established?

C ontent validity is ensuring that a concept, even a complex unobservable concept like anomie, is comprehensively measured with the survey questions chosen to represent the construct. If the construct is measured completely, then high content validity exists. There are several steps researchers can take to ensure content validity.

Beginning with a deep reading of all existing research on the concept to provide the varying dimensions and definitions of each dimension that makes up the concept. Additionally, the measures or survey questions used by other researchers alongside a critique of how well those measures worked allow us to do two things. First, identify completely all dimensions of the concept, and secondly, begin to create a list of all possible survey questions that attempt to measure the various dimensions and subdimensions of the concept.

For example, "anomie" has been defined as the breakdown of connection between the individual and society. Durkheim used it in his book, *Suicide*, to reflect the difference in moral standards between individuals and the larger community as major societal changes occur. Others have called it normlessness, while others see it as a form of social disorder.

Once all aspects of the concept are understood, survey questions should be developed to measure all aspects of the concept. Existing survey questions can be used, but it may be that there are none or the ones that exist aren't very valid. Then researchers must design their own survey questions to measure the concept. In these cases, it is useful to request assistance from experts in the concept to look over the set of survey questions and provide input as to the completeness of content coverage.

More questions? See questions 35, 36, and 43.

What Is Criterion Validity?

C riterion validity assesses the accuracy of our survey questions to some established, independent instrument that measures the same underlying concept. If the two correlate highly, then we have validated our survey question measures with the instrument. For example, if we want to predict who will do well in college, then we want to measure college success, meaning grade point average (GPA). What is a good criterion for this? Colleges and universities tend to use the SAT or ACT scores for this. If SAT scores and college GPA are highly and positively correlated, then SAT scores are a good criterion.

Use of SAT scores as a criterion for future GPA is an example of predictive criterion validity because the criterion is measured prior to the outcome we want to validate. Criteria can be contemporaneous or concurrent as well. An example of a concurrent validity test would be to validate survey questions on drinking behavior with a blood alcohol test. Of course, the problem with this criterion is that the blood test won't show much unless the survey and blood test are conducted when and where people drink. Blood alcohol dissipates over time.

Criteria must be chosen carefully, of course, for this type of validation to work. The criterion needs to be representative of the concept or phenomenon under consideration. If we have access to the criterion, why is it not being used instead of the survey questions devised? The problem is that for most social science concepts and phenomenon, there are no good criteria we can use. In the cases where we might find one, it is often too expensive or difficult to use. In addition, the more abstract the concept, the less likely there is to be a criterion that adequately represents it. For these reasons, criterion validity is rarely useful or applicable for most concepts in the social sciences.

More questions? See questions 43, 44, and 46.

What Is Construct Validity?

C onstruct validity is another way to determine how accurately our survey question measures the concept. To ascertain construct validity, we look to theory to tell us how our concept ought to be associated with other concepts. We then test these theoretical relations with our survey measures. For example, in the case of Durkheim's theoretical concept, anomie, those individuals who experience anomie, meaning a lack of connection with his or her community, will be more likely to commit suicide. Assuming we have the data, using our measures of anomie and additional measures of suicide ideation, meaning thoughts about committing suicide, we can correlate them. To the extent these two measured concepts are correlated, we have some evidence of construct validity.

We want to demonstrate both convergent and discriminant forms of construct validity. Convergent validity is similar to the idea of concurrent criterion validity in that it assesses the association between two survey questions that roughly measure the same concept. Neither survey question is a criterion measure, however. To the extent these two different measures of the same concept are highly correlated, we have added more evidence of construct validity. Recall that a high correlation can be either positive or negative. If we can demonstrate convergent validity across multiple construct domains, that provides greater confidence in measurement validity.

Discriminant validity returns to theory and asks, *What concepts are not associated with our concept of interest*? In other words, rather than looking to what other concepts theoretically it should be related to, also look to what it shouldn't be associated with. Anomie, which is about a lack of connection to community, should not be associated with transportation to work. Both forms of construct validity lead to confidence that the survey question measures the concept.

Exploratory Factor Analysis is an advanced statistical technique that is becoming the standard tool in confirming construct validity by assessing the common variation across a number of survey questions. It is beyond the scope of this text, however.

More questions? See questions 43, 44, and 45.

What Is Measurement Reliability, and How Is It Established?

"Measurement reliability" is defined as consistency in responses to survey questions. We want a survey question to provide reliable data. That is, if the same person answered the same question multiple times, we would get consistent and dependable responses every time. Unlike validity, accuracy is less the aim than is consistency. However, if a survey question is unreliable, then it also will be invalid or full of error.

One type of reliability is called test–retest. This tests the reliability of results after repeated administration of the same question. A reliable survey question should produce a similar response over two points in time. There needs to be enough time between the repeated tests so that memory is not being tested, but not so much time that the answer to the survey question could realistically change. This is limited because people might remember from one test to another. Alternate form reliability is a test–retest method with a different version of the survey question offered at time 2. The questions should vary only slightly in the wording. With both of these tests, it is impossible to distinguish real change from lack of reliability.

Split halves method is to treat the survey questions as if they were on alternative forms. Split the total set of measures that reflect the concept in some way, such as odds in one group and even-numbered questions in the other. Then correlate the scores on the two halves with each other to see if there is reliability. This works well, but may have the problem that different measures of reliability might vary depending on how the items are split.

The internal consistency method is the most commonly used method to assess reliability, and Cronbach's alpha is the most used reliability measure. This measure of reliability is based on both the average inter-item (survey questions) correlation and the number of items used. This tells us that reliability can be increased by using more rather than fewer survey questions to measure a concept. Most statistical software packages can easily calculate Cronbach's alpha.

More questions? See questions 43, 48, and 49.

48

What Is Measurement Error?

"Measurement error" is defined as the difference between a participant's "true" answer to a survey question and the answer they actually give (as opposed to standard deviation or standard error, which are measures of dispersion about the mean of a variable). A difference can happen because the question fails to measure the concept well (random error) or is biased in some way perhaps through using leading language (systematic error). If the survey question doesn't measure the concept well, we can expect that the error will be random—meaning that some people will underreport and others will overreport their true answer. Since responses are equally likely to be both over- and underreported, the error is assumed, over a large group of respondents, to net out to zero error. However, while it may net to zero, it will affect reliability or the consistency of our survey questions' ability to measure our concepts. Therefore, we want to minimize this form of error.

With biased or leading questions, however, all the error will be in the same direction, leading to systematic measurement error. It affects all participants in the same way through a skewed survey question. There are other ways to add systematic error into the study. Nonresponse bias can be systematic. For example, if some survey questions are complex, it may be that people with lower levels of education are less likely to try to answer them. This would mean that the group that doesn't answer this set of questions has lower education in common and that they are systematically different in terms of education with those who did answer the questions. These questions then are systematically biased toward responses of the better educated.

Questionnaire bias and interviewer bias can also lead to systematic measurement bias. If the questionnaire is too long, not organized well, too confusing, or too cluttered, there will be systematic differences in who can make their way through the survey and who cannot. In interviewer-administered surveys, characteristics of the interviewers can lead or influence responses to questions in systematic ways. Systematic bias leads to invalid measurement.

More questions? See questions 43, 47, and 49.

49

How Can Measurement Error Be Minimized?

There will always be some random measurement error; that is unavoidable. There should never be systematic measurement error in the study because that will make it a flawed study.

The best way to minimize measurement error is to devote considerable time and attention to the design of the survey questions. Follow all the rules of writing the best, unbiased, or non leading questions possible. Provide an exhaustive and mutually exclusive set of response categories. If a single question is too complicated, break it down into two or three simple questions. Write good, clear instructions for each question, and make sure to provide definitions to terms that anyone, regardless of education or background, can understand. Make sure to engage in every effort to ensure a high response rate (see Part 6), including assurances of confidentiality or anonymity.

Keep the questionnaire well organized and uncluttered, meaning lots of white space. Have the questions flow in a clear and organized manner. Make sure the questions are simple, specific, and direct. Reduce the burden on respondents by using consistent language, instructions, and types of questions. Make the questionnaire as short as possible while still being able to answer the research question.

If using a phone or face-to-face administration, make sure all interviewers are well trained, understand the survey and the questions, and know how the researcher wants the questions presented to the participants. Try to avoid interviewer fatigue by not overworking them. Make sure the interview takes place when there are no distractions such as children crying for dinner in the background. In fact, make sure the participants are in a quiet and private place so that they will give truthful answers. All of these steps will minimize systematic error.

More questions? See questions 38, 43, and 48.

How Can Pretesting and Pilot Testing Improve Reliability and Validity?

Once a draft of the survey is complete, the process of assessing reliability and validity begins. Pretesting is having group of experts take the survey and then using a Likert scale set of items to answer whether or not each survey question represents the underlying concept (strongly represents to weakly represents). This will highlight where there are some problematic survey questions that need more work. This type of pretesting will improve face and content validity. This can reduce measurement error. Conduct a pretest prior to the pilot test.

A pilot test, sometimes called a feasibility study, is a rehearsal of the entire study from administration to data entry and analysis. A pilot test can use between 30 and 100 participants. The pilot should be conducted on a broad cross section of the target population (if used for the pilot, participants are ineligible for the full study). This is especially important for large and complex studies with many moving parts. The purpose is to identify problems in the data management plan, coding decisions, and even data entry plans, and correct them prior to implementing the full study. It can be helpful in determining if staff training was appropriate or if more training is needed. Recruitment approaches can be assessed for their effectiveness, and new approaches can be added as needed. Incentives can be assessed for their adequacy. Give the pilot test plenty of time so that analysis of data can be fully conducted.

Once pilot testing is complete, the raw data can be used to conduct preliminary reliability and validity testing, which is important for finalizing the survey questionnaire. At this stage, adding, dropping, or rewriting questions can be decided based on findings from data analysis.

More questions? See questions 43, 48, and 49.

Conducting the Survey

6

51

Once the Survey Is Designed, How Is the Survey Conducted?

S urveys can be administered either by using a trained interviewer or self-administered by having the participants fill out the survey by themselves. Self-administered surveys can be conducted either using pen and paper (mailed) or online (web based or e-mailed). Interviewer-administered surveys can be conducted over the phone, or face to face. They can also be administered using a computer with the survey coded into a survey program.

We make decisions on which administration method to use (see Table 51.1) based on (1) resources available, (2) who the participants are, (3) how complicated the survey is, and (4) what response rate we need. It takes fewer resources to have a survey be self-administered rather than administered by trained interviewers. Not all participants have access to computers which limits online administration. Studies of low-income communities, immigrants, or children may have language barriers, and

Table 51.1 Pros and Cons of Survey Administration Types

	Pros	Cons
Pen and Paper, Mailed	Inexpensive; can reach a lot of people	Low response rate, must be a simple survey, data entry needed
Telephone	Can have complicated survey; can reach low literacy participants	Expensive; can't access all phones; low response rate,
Face-to-Face	Highest response rate; can have complicated survey; can reach low literacy participants	Data entry needed unless computer used; expensive
Web-Based	Inexpensive; can have complicated survey	Low response rate; not everyone has a computer

therefore, an interviewer-administered survey makes more sense. The more complicated the survey—with questions being skipped or complex concepts used, the more likely it is you will want an interviewer-administered survey.

The response rate, again, is the ratio of those who completed the survey to those selected into the sample. We are looking for a response rate of about 70%. It is getting harder and harder to achieve a 70% response rate. Self-administered surveys tend to have very low response rates. Telephone surveys, with the advent of cell phones, are also likely to produce low response rates. Face-to-face interviewer-administered surveys tend to produce the highest response rates, but at the highest cost.

For any given survey study, researchers must balance their resources with the needs of the participants, the research goals, and the complexity of the survey questionnaire. In other words, they should choose the administration type that will maximize response rates for the available resources.

More questions? See questions 4, 31, and 52.

52

How Often Can We Contact the Sample to Get Them to Participate?

While it is possible that participants will complete the survey after the first interaction with the study, this is not very common. Most will junk the e-mail or snail mail the first time they receive it. People are busy and receive a lot of junk mail, which means they may not see the importance of your study right away.

This means multiple contacts with the participants are needed. Prior to beginning data collection, think through how many contacts are feasible in terms of costs. Also, think ethically about when the line is crossed between diligence and stalking the sample. Then, stick to the number of contacts because the researcher's desire to get participants should not outweigh the rights of participants to not participate. For instance, if conducting a mail survey, how many surveys can the researcher afford to print and mail out? Then, at what point will additional mailings upset the participants? Perhaps limit mailings to three or four. Make sure a few weeks pass between mailings to give people time to respond. E-mailing surveys is inexpensive; however, too many contacts may feel coercive to participants. Treat e-mail contacts as similar to mail contacts. Limit them to about four, and again let some time pass between e-mailings.

For a phone survey or face-to-face survey, each of which is far more expensive, how many contacts are affordable? Face-to-face interactions make it harder for participants to say no. Two or three contacts should be sufficient to obtain a high response rate without being coercive. Phone contacts are difficult because people often aren't home or no longer accept calls from unknown numbers. Calling on various days and at various times could be appropriate without feeling coercive to participants. Therefore, perhaps up to 30 calls may be needed to get a participant on the phone. Change up the contacts too. If sending out mail or e-mail contacts, don't send the same message each time because it clearly didn't work the first time. Change up any voice-messaging scripts between calls to attract attention.

More questions? See questions 9, 51, and 53.

QUESTION

53

How Are the Potential Members of the Sample Contacted?

S ending a survey to participants without introduction or advanced warning is not very successful. Depending on how the survey will be administered, an introductory letter or postcard may prepare the way for the survey and ensure a better response rate. The message on the letter or postcard should be persuasive; it needs to convince the sample members of the relevance or importance of the study and that participating will not be a waste of their time. This can also be accomplished with a cover letter attached to the survey.

If you have the resources and/or are conducting a local survey, a face-to-face interaction is another way to connect with the sample. It is easier to build rapport face-to-face and harder for the participant to turn you down. A phone call might be appropriate if you have a phone number, resources, and a national sample. However, people routinely avoid calls from unknown numbers, so an introductory letter or postcard might improve the chances of your call being answered.

In fact, sending a postcard announcing the study prior to mailing, e-mailing, phoning, or knocking on doors might be the best first contact. A postcard that is bright and colorful, or uses a story-telling graphic while announcing the study is more likely to garner interest. It also tells the participants to be on the lookout for the survey mail, e-mail, phone call, or visit that is coming in the next week.

Contacting the participants is just the first step. Persuading the sample to participate is the harder problem and deserves a great deal of time and attention to get right.

More questions? See questions 51, 52, and 54.

QUESTION

54

How Are the Sample Members Persuaded to Participate?

Participants are persuaded by caring for the survey's purpose. Start by "branding" the study. Find the words that will trigger interest in the topic and will make the participants want to complete the survey. This is not easy. In the early 2000s, every survey used the phrase "let your voice be heard" or some variant of that. It is now overused. Plus, people use social media these days to make their voices heard.

The example in Figure 54.1 is a transportation study focusing on traffic. It's branded, "We're going places," and it solicits help. These are strong messages for a topic that is not extremely important. The graphic shows a traffic jam

---

Figure 54.1

Dear Resident,

Next week you will receive an important survey on Atlanta traffic. You have been chosen at random to represent your community, and your opinion is very important to us.

As you may know, Atlanta has a national reputation for heavy traffic but is working on ways to make it better and we want to hear about real traffic experiences and attitudes from various Atlanta residents.

[RECIPIENT NAME]
[Recipient Address]
[City, ST ZIP Code]

Completing the survey is one way in which your voice can be included in new transportation improvements. To complete the survey online, please go to this link: linktomygreatsurvey.com and type in this code: XXXXXXX

WE'RE GOING PLACES
and we need your help!

---

and personalizes it by asking, *Could this be you?* The GSU logo legitimizes the study as real research. On the reverse side, the study is briefly explained and connection with the sample members is attempted by asking for their traffic experiences and stating the importance of hearing from them to improve traffic conditions.

The branding messages in the postcards should be included in all correspondence such as the cover letter and the survey itself and any interactions with sample members.

More questions? See questions 52, 53, and 55.

What Should Be Included in a Cover Letter?

The cover letter introduces the research and the researcher to the participants; it is an invitation to participate. The quality of the data recovered from the survey may depend on how good the cover letter is. Therefore, create a good cover letter for all survey administration types.

The cover letter should start with the invitation. It should show appreciation for participating in the study. Spend time explaining the nature of the study, and how long it will take to complete. Explain who has been selected to participate and why. Include how the participants' contact information was obtained because that can make participants nervous. Include any information such as sponsoring university and that the research has ethical approval from an institutional review board (IRB), which will help legitimize the study.

All of the above informs the participants, but it is not persuasive in encouraging participation. How can researchers explain the importance of the study that will connect with the participants? Brand the study so that all communications send the same message, such as in the postcard in Q54. Ask for the participants' help. Explain that this is a way for participants' voices to be heard. Some studies find humor might work, such as listing the top 10 reasons to participate. Ensure anonymity or confidentiality of responses. Keep it short and to the point; don't waste participants' time with more than one page.

In a time when spam mail is abundant and often is tossed out, and spam e-mail is automatically junked, personalizing the cover letter or e-mail will help it from being tossed. Use a return address that is legitimate—such as a university address or business address. Sign it and include information so participants can contact the researcher with any questions. Avoid using JavaScript or other e-mail features that will get tagged by a spam filter.

More questions? See questions 53, 54, and 56.

What Other Strategies Can Increase Survey Participation?

A n incentive is helpful to create a sense of obligation on the part of the participant. Don't think of the incentive as "paying" for the participants' time, but rather as a token of appreciation. Prepaid incentives work best. It should be a small amount that doesn't feel coercive. Institutional review boards (IRBs) carefully monitor the incentive amounts for research. If the amount is large enough to compel respondents to participate, IRBs will not sponsor the research and expect the study to reduce the incentive amount.

Money is not the only incentive. Swag, such as bags, magnets, and T-shirts, can also be an incentive to complete the survey. The Wisconsin Longitudinal Study, which has been interviewing the high school graduates from the class of 1957 for over 50 years, sent all participants a CD of the greatest hits from 1957 as an incentive in 2005. This incentive evoked nostalgic memories, continued with the branding of the study, and created a bond between the study and the participants.

Offering to share findings from the study with the participants can also be convincing. If respondents find the topic compelling, they will appreciate seeing firsthand what comes from participating in the study. The report sent to participants should be very formal and professional looking, but without the jargon and statistical methods that dominate academic writing. It should be written in everyday English and be easy to read and understand by the lay person.

The survey itself can be used to inspire participation. The first question should be appealing to participants through either its importance or engaging nature. Make sure the questionnaire is short and easy for participants to get through. If the survey is overly burdensome, participants will stop taking it.

A well-thought-out plan to engage participants should result in a high response rate.

More questions? See questions 53, 54, and 55.

How Do We Keep Track of Who Has and Has Not Participated?

If the plan is to contact participants multiple times and perhaps use multiple methods, it might get confusing about who has been contacted, how they've been contacted, and what is the result of that contact. Therefore, it behooves the researcher to set up some files such as a spreadsheet to keep track of contacts and participation.

A simple spreadsheet might include the participants' name, unique identifier used on the survey, contact information, date of first contact, outcome of first contact, and so on for all contacts. The spreadsheet should be updated regularly so that multiple contacts do not happen for participants who have either already completed the survey or refused. There is no point in bothering people not to mention wasting scarce resources unnecessarily. Make sure all names are removed from the data or spreadsheet at the end of the study for privacy.

It is important to determine what the outcomes will be ahead of time. Clearly, "complete" is the most desired outcome, but a "refusal" should be marked as well. If there are eligibility criteria, it's possible that a participant might be "ineligible." Participants might die between sampling and administration of the survey, or they might move outside the study zone. For address-based studies, the home may be vacant or the address might be bad. Phone numbers might be out of service. Some refusals are a hard "no" to participate (do not bother me again), while others can be considered "soft," meaning they are busy now but try again later.

Once data collection is complete, this spreadsheet can be used to create a final disposition. This can tell us what percent is complete, ineligible, refused, or with whom we had made no contact. Based on this information, the response rates can be calculated.

More questions? See questions 51, 52, and 49.

58

How Do We Conduct a Longitudinal Study?

Longitudinal panel studies interview the same participants multiple times over several years. This means participants first have to be persuaded to participate, but then have to be persuaded to remain with the study over time. Attrition, or dropping out of the study after participating a time or two, becomes a serious problem. Branding the study and getting the sample to identify with the study is more important than ever. More time and attention should be paid to this part of the data-collection effort. Another issue is that people move and sometimes move quite far. Researchers need to stay in contact with participants between survey administrations or hire a service that can locate participants. Social security numbers are a great way to be able to relocate people if they have moved. Unfortunately, many people are leery of identity theft, and are no longer willing to share their social security numbers. Sending regular study updates and policy implications of the research can help the participants feel pride of accomplishment as well as maintain contact.

Tracking participation can also become more complicated. Not all participants respond to every survey administration. One part of the tracking procedure would be to find out why some did not participate the last time. Perhaps they were incarcerated or in the hospital the last time but now are out and available to participate again. Others may no longer be eligible or no longer living, in which case, you would not add them back into the tracking spreadsheet. Tracking the survey versions adds to the complexity. You might want a separate sheet for each wave of the longitudinal study. Some prefer to use a relational database to keep track of participants.

Essentially, the work is the same for both a cross-sectional survey and a panel survey, but more resources are needed for each data-collection activity with a panel design.

More questions? See questions 51, 54, and 57.

59

What Other Survey Administration Issues May Arise?

While data collection is ongoing, there are several monitoring activities that may be helpful. If the survey is interviewer administered, then ongoing training of interviewers and debriefing of interviewers in regular field meetings will keep the training fresh in the interviewers' minds and raise any new issues. If the survey is self-administered, checking to see if respondents are getting through it fine is important. If many stop at the same place, this may point out survey difficulties that did not arise during the pretesting or pilot testing. If there is a major problem in the survey, making a change and noting the date will allow the researcher to determine how that change affected survey responses.

If not already planned out, planning for the post survey collection is the next task. What computer capacities are available? Is there sufficient data storage space? Is the data storage place safe and secure from hacking? What data back-up plans are in place? Given that computer hardware and software technologies are rapidly changing, are there adequate resources to keep the computer systems up to date throughout the study period? It is important to have the ability to store data in several locations. Computer hard drives fail all the time. It is very expensive to try to salvage a hard drive. Obtaining cloud storage is simple and inexpensive, as are flash drives. Fortunately, computer technology is very inexpensive these days, and there are plenty of options to store and safeguard data.

Make sure whatever software is used to collect the data is compatible with the software being used to analyze the data. If using a mail method and data must be entered by hand, make sure to set up an easy-to-use data entry form, and again, that this form is compatible with the data analysis software. Make sure to save some resources to hire data entry personnel.

More questions? See questions 4, 61, and 62.

How Do We Take Care of Survey Participants?

A benefit of the survey is that it is cost effective. That is, adding another question to the survey or adding another person to the study will not add much to the cost of conducting the survey. However, we are only thinking about our costs and our needs in conducting the research. What about the needs of the participants? We do not want to impose a large burden on our participants. Therefore, the survey should be as short as possible. Research on conducting survey research found that a 10-minute survey is about the right size. This works for a telephone or interview based survey. For a written or online survey, this translates to about four or five pages. Anything more than that is quite burdensome to participants.

Other ways in which we can reduce the burden on the participants is having an easy-to-follow survey structure with good instructions. If there are a lot of attitude statements with a Likert set of response categories (strongly disagree to strongly agree), do not scatter them all over the survey, but put them all together to make answering them easier. Do not have too many different types of Likert scale items. This gets confusing. Stick to just a few types, and again, make sure the instructions are clear.

Make sure the survey has plenty of space between questions and is consistent in the presentation of questions and response categories. This consistency will be a form of training for the participants, and they will know what to expect and how to answer each question.

If there are sensitive questions, remind the participants of confidentiality. If it is an interviewer-conducted survey, perhaps allow participants to answer the sensitive questions without the interviewer. Hand over the tablet or computer. End the survey on a positive note. Leave the participants reflecting on something positive and happy related to the topic of the survey, and hopefully that feeling will be associated with the survey.

More questions? See questions 54, 56, and 59.

Entering and Cleaning the Data

7

61

Do We Need to Plan Ahead for Data Entry, Cleaning, and Analysis?

I t is important to plan ahead for how to handle the data once it is collected. Many researchers put off planning the data entry, cleaning, and documenting until after data is collected. This is not the most efficient way to do things. A little preplanning or a pilot test (see Q50) will help the post–data collection process run very smoothly.

Several of these post–data collection tasks actually impinge upon the survey itself. For example, in the response categories to survey questions, do we want to allow participants to refuse to answer or to mark "don't know"? If we do not include them, participants might simply skip the question—leave it blank. If refusals differ from don't knows, we will want to include these response options.

The preplanning also involves thinking about how to identify individual participants without using their name or social security number. How big of a unique identifier number do we need? If the sample is over 1,000, then we will need at least five digits. For some studies, we may want the identifier to do more than uniquely identify the participants. For example, for a mixed-administration-mode survey project, all online surveys can have unique identifiers that begin with 1 and all mail surveys can have unique identifiers that start with a 2.

Once these decisions are made, we are ready to move on to data entry, or if the data were entered by an online survey program, to data cleaning.

More questions? See questions 4, 62, and 63.

My Data Is Collected. Now What Do I Do?

The hard part is over, but there is still a good bit of work left to do. First, the data must be organized in such a way that it can be used to answer the research question. Second, the data must be cleaned and prepped for analysis. Third, the analysis is conducted, and tables, graphics, and figures are created (Parts 8 & 9). Lastly, the data are written up in a report or article in which the research question is posed and answered with supporting empirical evidence (Part 10).

The organization of the data starts with data entry. Data entry transforms each survey question into a variable to be used in a statistical database. The variable will need a name and a variable label. Variable labels help to remind us exactly what is included in the variable. Each response option will be given a number. It is the number that makes up the data. To remind ourselves what text the numbers represent, we assign value labels to each number.

For example, in Figure 62.1, there is a survey question. For this question, the variable name could be Q1. In this way the data in the final dataset can be matched to the original dataset when needed. An appropriate variable label could be *Spends too much time in traffic.* The numbers 1, 2, 3, 4, and 5 could be assigned to each successive response category. For data entry purposes, this example would get a 4, as it is the checked response. Each value could then be assigned its label: 4 = Agree.

If using an online survey administration program, all of this work takes place when setting up the survey. If not, paper surveys need to be entered by hand once complete.

Figure 62.1 Survey Question Example

Q1 How much do you agree or disagree with the following statement: I spend too much time in Traffic. (Check the box that matches your level of agreement.)

☐ Strongly disagree ☐ Disagree ☐ Neutral √ Agree ☐ Strongly Agree

More questions? See questions 61, 63, and 64.

63

How Do We Do Data Entry?

P rior to converting each survey question into a variable in the database, it is helpful to code a paper version of the survey. On one copy of the survey, first write the variable names next to each survey question. Use a consistent variable naming scheme—usually, the question number. Statistical software packages give 25 character spaces for variable names, so names that reflect the meaning of the question can be used. However, shorter variable names will mean fewer errors and typos during the analysis phase. Put the correct numeric value next to each response category if it is not already there. Note which variables are gateway variables and which additional variables are included in the skip patterns. Also note any other unusual type of survey question such as a *choose all that apply*, a *specify other*, and open-ended questions. Figure out how to handle these questions prior to entering the data.

Start data entry by creating a data entry skeleton. Use a spreadsheet program or SPSS to set up the skeleton. On the top row, put each variable name in a single column until all variables are included. The variable ID, for unique identifier, should go in the very first column. Next, enter each survey in a single row from ID to the last variable. Also write each ID number given on each survey in case you need to refer back to the survey ever. If the sample size is 100, then 100 rows will be used for the participants or "cases," as participants are called once turned into a dataset. The next step is to convert the spreadsheet into a statistical software package. Once in the software package, syntax or the specific software language can be used to add variable labels and value labels (see Q62). At this point the dataset has been created.

More questions? See questions 62, 64, and 65.

64

What Issues Might Arise With Data Entry?

There are a few things to look out for during data entry. First, some participants might not answer all the questions. This is called item nonresponse. A decision needs to be made on how to handle this. Generally, a code for "refused to answer" is created, such as −1, and then when a question is not answered, the code for "refused to answer" is entered. But that isn't the only reason an item might not be answered. Some questions have built-in skip patterns. For example, let's say a survey has 10 questions about smoking behavior, and the first question asks if the participant smokes at all. If the participant answers no, then that participant is "skipped" past the other nine smoking questions. In this case, a "refused to answer" would not be appropriate. Rather, a "not applicable" code would be more appropriate. Give "not applicable" a code of −2. Or, if the survey question is asking about opinions or knowledge of some sort and the participant doesn't know how to answer that, "refused to answer," again, is not appropriate. A "don't know" response makes more sense. It is helpful to include a "don't know" option and a "refuse to answer" option with the questions for respondents to choose when completing the survey.

Another problem is when participants choose more than one answer or pick up parts of two response categories. It is impossible for the researcher to know what the participant meant to choose. But there is some information provided; we know what answers were not chosen. The most conservative fix for this problem is to assign a missing value, such as "refused to answer," but these cases are different from true refusals; therefore, a new missing code, such as "unclear response," can be created. Alternatively, some *a priori* systematic rule can be created on how to handle these cases. For example, each data entry person can flip a coin; if it comes up heads, then the first problem case gets the top category; if its tails, then the bottom category is chosen. Then the next time it happens, choose the opposite category. Keep alternating top and bottom until done. This adds variation into the data. This is less conservative but builds on what information is available.

More questions? See questions 63, 65, and 66.

What Types of Survey Questions Are Difficult to Enter Into the Database?

There are three types of questions that are difficult to enter into the database. The first is a "choose all answers that apply" type of survey question. We can only give one numeric value per variable. Therefore, if there is an "all that apply" type question, create a separate variable for each response category. Each of these variables will have two numeric values: 1 for "chose this answer" and 2 for "did not choose this answer." In the boxed example below, five variables would be created. Q2a would be for cigarettes. Q2a would get a 1 if a participant chose it and a 2 if the participant did not choose it. Q2b would be the variable name for cigars.

Q2 What tobacco products have you tried … (choose all that apply)

☐ cigarettes ☐ cigars ☐ pipes ☐ dip/chew ☐ cigarillos

The other two types deal with text responses such as open-ended questions and "other, please specify" responses. My advice with open-ended questions is to type in the responses verbatim and code the variables later in the data cleaning stages. We cannot perform statistical analyses on text, which is why we will have to code the responses into numeric values at some point. The reason to include them verbatim is so that we have a record of the answer in a database form. We can go back to the original answer later if we find an error or want to add a new code.

"Other, please specify" questions should become a separate variable and the text responses recorded exactly. They are easier to code than open-ended items, but it is best to retain a record of the original answer in the database. In the boxed example on race, someone who is biracial might check the box for other and then type in *Black* and *Asian*. The variable Q3 would be given the response of 5 for the fifth box. A new variable named "Q3_*text*" would be created and *Black and Asian* could be typed in as the other response type.

Q3 Would you say you are … (race/ethnicity)

☐ White ☐ Black ☐ Asian ☐ Hispanic ☐ Other, please specify _____

More questions? See questions 64, 66, and 67.

QUESTION

66

What Is a Codebook, and Why Is It Important?

A codebook is a separate document from the dataset, often in Word or Excel, that contains critical information for data users. *It is very important.* First of all, it matches the survey questions to the variable names listed in the dataset. It provides descriptions of what all the variables represent. It also provides secondary information such as the full text of the questionnaire items, variable labels, values, and matching value labels. Most computer-assisted survey programs will automatically generate a codebook, but if not, they are simple to create. An example of a codebook is found in Table 66.1 below. The first column tells us where to find the variable in the dataset. Column 2 provides the variable name. The third column provides the variable label, values, and value labels. For Q2, the only value label given is for missing values because the ages 18 to 65 have meaning already.

Remember that in general, each question in the survey should have its own unique variable (column in the dataset), and each participant should have his or her own unique identification number (and row in the dataset). We can use the creation of the codebook to ensure that this is the case. Some codebooks include skip patterns or frequencies to help new users. Aim for consistency in variable naming, variable labeling, and values and value labels, but also in the information included in the codebook. This will make the entire process easier. The goal of data cleaning and documenting with codebooks is for clarity and transparency so that anyone new to the project will easily and quickly learn how to navigate the dataset using the codebook.

Table 66.1 Codebook Example		
Position	**Variable Name**	**Variable Label, Values, and Value labels**
1	**CASEID**	**Unique Identification Number**
2	**Q1**	**Which of the following best describes your sex?** **1 = Male** **2 = Female**
3	**Q2**	**How old are you? Valid responses range from 18–65** **R = Refused**

More questions? See questions 4, 61, and 62.

What Other Sorts of Documentation Are Needed, and Why?

The codebook is the most important document for a study because it connects the survey questionnaire and the dataset. There are at least two other sets of documents that may be helpful to create and maintain. The first is the syntax file used to enter and clean the data. Syntax is the language used to code in statistical software packages. Comments can be used throughout the syntax to explain what is happening in each set of syntax. Dates can be useful in the syntax comments as well to help us remember when different parts of the syntax were run on the data.

The syntax, even without comments, provides a transparency trail of all variable manipulations that happened. If during the analyses stage, something looks strange or funny about a variable, we can scroll through the syntax and see everything that was done to that variable to see if an error was made. If so, the syntax can be fixed and rerun and all datasets easily re-created.

Another type of documentation that is beneficial is a technical report. The technical report lists every dataset in order from raw data entry to analysis datasets, what they are named, and where they are located. It will also list the name and location of each syntax file used to create the next dataset. Each set of syntax should have a brief description that includes which variables were manipulated, what was done to them, the date it was done, and who was the author of the syntax. A file like this allows us to know how far back we need to go to correct a problem, how many datasets to re-create, and how many sets of syntax to rerun, then where to re-save all the incorrect datasets with the new, corrected dataset. Having the author's name allows us to contact the author and make sure that what looks strange about a variable is truly a mistake and not how it is supposed to look. These files will make working with the data easier and will increase clarity and transparency.

More questions? See questions 61, 62, and 63.

What Is Data Cleaning?

Data cleaning is the process of checking all variables in the dataset diagnostically as well as cosmetically to ensure all variables are ready for analysis. Start by noting which variables are string variables (text responses) versus numeric variables. Check to see if the string variables ought to be string variables, meaning are they open-ended questions or "other specify" response variables? If yes, set them aside. If no, convert the string variable to be numeric. This is easily accomplished in SAS or STATA by adding 0 ($Q12n = Q12 + 0$), and in SPSS by using the "recode into new variable" option from the drop-down menu. In Excel, format the column.

With the numeric variables, we start and end with a frequency on each variable. A frequency provides a listing of each response category in the first column followed by the count of all responses in each category, and the percent of the total responses in that category in the next columns. The last two columns provide cumulative counts and percentages. If the variable is a continuous variable—either ratio or interval measurement—, then the meaning of the numbers are the numbers. For example, age is continuous, and a value of 25 would mean age 25. For these types of variables, we are looking for (1) variable label—Does it have one, and is it correct? (2) implausible values—values that are too small or too large given what we know about the sample; (3) Is there variation in the responses? and (4) Are there any missing values, and if there are, how are they coded, if at all? For binary or ordinal numeric variables, we add a fifth thing to look for (5) Are there correct value labels? When we find a problem, we go back to the original survey or data to see if the problem can be fixed. We use syntax to correct the problem: Run the syntax, and then run a final frequency on the variable to ensure that the syntax did in fact correct the problem. In the example in Table 68.1, we find no diagnostic problems

Table 68.1 Frequency of Variable Q1

Q1	Frequency	Percentage	Cum Count	Cum Percent
1	60	29.3%	60	29.3%
2	145	70.7%	205	100%

such as missing values or implausible values, or lack of variation, but there are no variable labels or value labels to tell us what this variable is and what 1 and 2 mean. Now we know what to fix.

More questions? See questions 66, 67, and 69.

How Are "Other Specify" Responses Coded?

"Other specify" response options in questions allow more flexibility for participants. Some categories are given, but one category is open, allowing participants to say whatever they want. An example would be Q3 below asking about race. If none of the given categories apply, participants can choose the "other" box and then write in what that other is.

Q3 Would you say you are … (race/ethnicity)

☐ White ☐ Black ☐ Asian ☐ Hispanic ☐ Other, please
specify _____

To code the "other specify" responses, start by determining what numeric value is assigned to the "other" category. In the case of variable, Q3, the numeric value would be 5. We can run a frequency of the text responses variable, Q3_text, where Q3 = 5 (getting the subset of Q3_text that applies). Our goal is to change the 5s in Q3 into a valid existing response if possible (1–4) or create new categories (6-n). For example, if a participant checks "other" and types in *Mexican*, then that participant can be recoded from 5 to 4 because Mexican fits into the category called Hispanic. If five participants say they are either *biracial* or *white & black*, then there are enough in that category to create a new code. These cases can all be recoded from 5 to 6 and category 6 can be given the value label, *Biracial*. If one person checks the "other" box and writes in *Native American*, then there aren't enough cases (we want at least five) to justify creating a new category. In this case, we leave the code as 5.

Once the syntax is written and run, we can run a crosstab of Q3 and Q3_text to make sure no mistakes were made. A crosstab is an *x* by *y* table with the first variable on the rows and the second variable on the columns. As demonstrated in Figure 69.1 below, *Mexican* was correctly put in the

Figure 69.1   Crosstab of Race by "Specify Other"

	White	Black	Asian	Hispanic	Other	Biracial
	1	2	3	4	5	6
.	124	0	0	0	0	0
.	0	57	0	0	0	0
.	0	0	15	0	0	0
.	0	0	0	23	0	0
Biracial	0	0	0	0	0	1
biracial	0	0	0	0	0	3
Mexican	0	0	0	1	0	0
Native American	0	0	0	0	1	0
White & Black	0	0	0	0	0	1

category *Hispanic* and the *biracial* and *white & black* responses were recoded as *biracial*.

More questions? See questions 65, 68, and 70.

70

How Are Open-Ended Questions Coded?

Open-ended question are wonderful for providing information in the participants' own words. Unfortunately, we need to turn them into numerical codes if we want to analyze the responses with the rest of the data. The coding process starts by reading all the open-ended responses carefully, several times. Over a couple of reads, themes may begin to emerge. This helps coders to understand how participants are understanding the question. Researchers often use either: NVivo, Atlas, dedoose, or NUDIST software to help code open-ended questions.

Next, develop an initial set of codes as a way of sorting or grouping the open-ended responses and code the open-ended responses. Do it in a spreadsheet with the codes in one column and text responses in another column. Make sure to include the text definitions of these codes. Sort the two columns by the initial codes.

The next step is to examine all the open-ended responses included in a single code and verify that they all belong together. If any don't really fit with the others, remove the code, and recode it. Some responses are really nonresponses to the question and can't really ever be coded. Give these responses a missing value code.

Repeat the sorting and coding until all responses that fit within a code have a single same code. Make a list of all the codes created, and number them from 1 to *n*. Create a definition of each code, and substantiate it with a couple of responses. Once the categories are created, create the new numeric variable, and give it a variable label and value label in the syntax. When this is done and the variable is created, run a crosstab like was done for the "other specify" recodes to ensure that all the text responses were coded into the correct category.

This is a long and arduous process. It helps sometimes to either have two people code independently, or have a second person code the final open-ended responses using the coding definitions created by the original coder. These two processes provide some reliability in coding.

More questions? See questions 65, 68, and 69.

Exploring the Data With Univariate Statistical Analysis

71

What Are the Goals of Data Analysis?

D ata analysis is the final step to answer the research question that started the survey project in the first place. Generally speaking, some form of statistical procedure involving one or more variables will be used. The first step is to explore all the variables in the dataset univariately meaning examining one variable at a time.

When there are a lot of observations on a single variable, it is sometimes hard to make sense of the data. Therefore, we want to summarize the data in some way. We do this with measures of central tendency and measures of variation. Measures of central tendency, such as mean, median, mode, and proportion in the modal category, provide us with the typical response. Measures of variance provide us with an understanding of the distribution of responses—how much they vary around that central response. Therefore, we will look at the standard deviation, the range, interquartile range, and proportion not in the modal category.

The next step is to examine bivariate relationships or associations between two variables. We might, for example, be interested in examining if people with higher levels of education earn more money compared to people with less education. Lastly, we move on to multivariable analyses, examining relationships between three or more variables. We might ask if the relationship between education and income is the same for men and women.

All statistical techniques used to analyze univariate, bivariate, and multivariable associations depend upon on how the variable is measured: ratio, interval, ordinal, or nominal. There are many statistical packages including Excel that can easily do any of these procedures. There are books, YouTube videos, and online help for using specific statistics programs, so we will not focus on that here. Also, a statistics textbook is recommended, as a course on statistics is beyond the scope of this text as well.

More questions? See questions 40, 72, and 73.

What Are Variables?

A variable is derived directly from each survey question. It varies from person to person within the survey, which is why it is called a variable. There are three basic types of variables: continuous (ratio and interval), ordinal, and nominal (see Q40). If a survey question asks about family income, then the variable, *faminc*, will consist of the dollar amount of income for each respondent. Family income is an example of a continuous variable. That is, the response categories are not fixed by the survey itself and can take on any positive number with up to two decimal places. Continuous variables lend themselves really well to mathematical operations.

Variables are measured as dichotomous and nominal if there are two response categories. A yes/no survey question provides us with dichotomous nominal variable. Numbers assigned to these types of questions are useful, but not meaningful arithmetically. A variable, such as religion, is nominal and has more than two categories (e.g., Catholic, Protestant, Judaism, Islam). There is no way to numerically organize categorical variables like religion; the numbers assigned to them are useful, but not meaningful. A respondent either is or is not Protestant.

Ordinal variables can be rank ordered such that we know some values are higher than others, but we do not know the distances between the values. Is the distance between small and medium the same as the distance between medium and large? If ordinal variables have many response categories (five or more), they are sometimes treated like continuous variables for univariate descriptive purposes. Others like to treat them like nominal variables for descriptive purposes. In any event, it is important to know how variables are measured in order to choose the correct statistical technique.

More questions? See questions 40, 62, and 71.

What Are Descriptive Statistics?

D escriptive statistics are a set of methods used to analyze data to under- stand and describe the sample. Univariate descriptive statistics describe each variable separately. In general, the best way to describe the data is to estimate the central tendency of a variable and a measure of dispersion (variation or standard deviation) around that central tendency—in other words, figuring out what is the typical response and how much respon- dents vary around that typical response. This is a way of summarizing the vast amount of information about each variable.

The measure of central tendency and dispersion will vary according to how each variable is measured. Table 73.1 lists the measures and tech- niques used for each variable type. For categorical and ordinal variables, the mode or most common response is the best measure of central ten- dency, usually presented as the proportion of sample in the modal category. To understand variation, estimating the proportion of responses in each

Table 73.1 Univariate Statistical Techniques for Each Type of Measured Variable					
Variable Measurement	Central Tendency	Measures of Variation (dispersion)	Plotting Distributions	Statistical Techniques	Example
Dichotomous Categorical	Mode	Proportions in each category	Bar charts	Frequency	Sex at birth
Categorical 3 + Categories	Mode	Proportions in each category	Bar charts	Frequency	Religions
Ordinal	Mode	Proportions in each category	Bar charts	Frequency	Grades (A, B, C)
Continuous	Mean or median	Standard deviation, variation, range, or interquartile range	Histograms, stem and leaf plots	Means	Income

category is best. For continuous variables, the mean and median are the best measures of central tendency.

These measures of central tendency are often called point estimates. The standard deviation is a good measure of variation. Also knowing the range—difference between first and last categories—provides information on variation. The interquartile range gives us the range between the top 25% and bottom 25% of a continuous distribution. If we want a graphical display of a variable's distribution, bar charts work best with categorical and ordinal variables, while histograms or stem and leaf patterns work best with continuous variables.

More questions? See questions 74, 75, and 76.

How Do We Estimate Central Tendency and Variation in Categorical and Ordinal Variables?

We use a frequency procedure to estimate central tendency and variation for categorical and ordinal variables. A frequency distribution provides a lot of information. For instance, a frequency distribution lists all possible values of the variables alongside the count and percentage of the sample that falls into that value. Table 74.1 provides an example of a frequency. Note that there are 565 respondents in the sample ($n = 565$).

The frequency distribution tells us that there are 396 white respondents in the sample, which comes to 70% (point estimate) of the total sample. This is the modal category. The mode is defined as the most frequently occurring value. In this sample, whites occur most frequently. To understand the racial distribution of the sample, we look at the other racial groups as well. African Americans make up an additional 20% of the sample, Asians 7%, and others are 3%.

Value (Label)	Frequency	Percentage	Cumulative Percentage
1 (White)	396	70%	70%
2 (African American)	113	20%	90%
3 (Asian)	40	7%	97%
4 (Other)	16	3%	100%
Total	565	100%	100%

Table 74.1 Frequency Distribution of Race

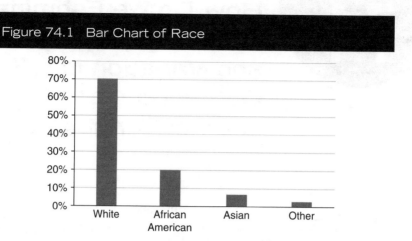

Figure 74.1 Bar Chart of Race

Frequency tables provide the information in numbers. Not everyone is good at reading tables of numbers. A bar chart is a good way to visually display the mode and variation. Figure 74.1 shows the mode consists of whites, and there is little racial variation in the sample.

More questions? See questions 71, 72, and 73.

How Do We Examine Central Tendency in Continuous Variables?

The arithmetic mean or median is used to estimate the central tendency or typical response of continuous variables. The mean is calculated as the sum of all responses divided by the number of responses: $mean\ of\ \bar{x} = \frac{\Sigma X}{n}$. The median is defined as the 50th percentile of the distribution of the variable from the lowest value to the highest value. If the distribution is broken up into four quarters (called quartiles) with 25% of the distribution in each, the median is at the end of the second quartile. It is the very central response. When the distribution of the continuous variable is perfectly symmetrical, the median and mean will be virtually identical.

We call this symmetrical distribution a bell curve. This is known as the normal distribution, which has important properties (see Q19). When there are some outliers, meaning really small or really large values that are very different from most of the responses, it will pull the distribution off symmetry (skew). In these cases, the mean and median will differ. If the difference between the two is large because there are many outliers, the median is the preferred measure of central tendency. If the distribution is symmetrical or close to symmetrical, the mean is the preferred measure.

Table 75.1 presents measures of central tendency for highest year of school completed, and grade point average (GPA). Highest year of school

Table 75.1 Measures of Central Tendency (n = 1,355)				
Variable	Mean	Median	Minimum	Maximum
Year of School Completed	13.4	12	1	20
GPA	2.95	3	1	4

completed has a mean of 13.4 years (point estimate) and a median of 12 (point estimate), so we know it is not symmetrically distributed. GPA, on the other hand, has a mean and median of ~3, which tells us the distribution is symmetrical.

More questions? See questions 72, 73, and 76.

How Do We Examine Variation in Continuous Variables When Using the Median?

When the median is the point estimate, then the range and the interquartile range are excellent measures of dispersion. The range is simply the difference between the first and last responses in the distribution. Providing information on the range provides the audience with a feel for the overall size of the distribution. It's good to use this with the mean also.

The interquartile range provides a measure of dispersion around the median. It is defined as the range of the distribution between the first and third quartiles. It is calculated as the variable's value at the 75th percentile minus the variable's value at the 25th percentile. This gives the range of values for the central 50th percentile of the variable's distribution. A good graphic to use to display central tendency and the range and interquartile range is a boxplot graph. Figure 76.1 presents a boxplot (box and

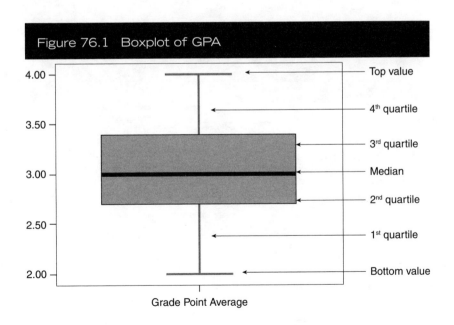

Figure 76.1   Boxplot of GPA

whisker plot) of grade point average (GPA). The thick line in the middle represents the median. The shaded box represents the interquartile range. The *T* and upside down *T*, called whiskers, represent the first and fourth quartile and provide the full range. If there are outliers, they appear as dots above and below the whiskers. This graph shows a normal bell curve distribution in the form of a boxplot.

More questions? See questions 73, 75, and 77.

How Do We Examine Variation in Continuous Variables When Using the Mean?

With the mean as the measure of central tendency, the variance and standard deviation are the best measures of dispersion to use. Again, measures of dispersion show us how spread out responses on a variable are. "Variance" is defined as the average squared deviation of each response from the mean of the variable (or $Var\,\bar{x} = \frac{\Sigma(x_i - \bar{x})^2}{N}$). The standard deviation is calculated as the square roaot of the variance. What's nice about the standard deviation is that it is in the same units as the mean: $SE\bar{x} = \sqrt{Var_{\bar{x}}}$.

If our variable is distributed normally (symmetrical bell curve), then the standard deviation provides important information about the distribution of responses under the bell curve. One hundred percent of all responses are under the bell distribution. Fifty percent are to the right of mean/median, and 50% are to the left of the mean/median. Sixty-eight percent of the sample are

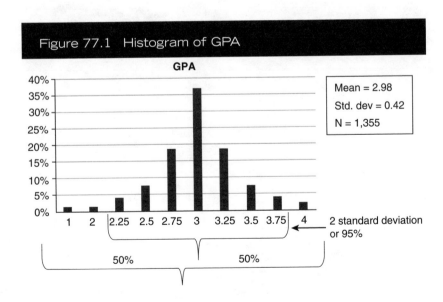

Figure 77.1 Histogram of GPA

within one standard deviation of the left and right of the mean, and 95% are within two standard deviations of the left and right of the mean.

A histogram is a graphic that gives a good demonstration of a variable's distribution. The histogram in Figure 77.1 shows the distribution of GPA for a sample of 1,355. The mean and median are at ~3, standard deviation is .42, and there is a clear bell curve, which happens when the data are normally distributed.

More questions? See questions 41, 75, and 76.

What Are Inferential Statistics?

While describing the sample is a good thing to do, we are more inter- ested in the larger population from which the sample was derived. Recall that the population is defined as the entire set of people about whom the researcher is interested. The sample is a subset of the entire population upon which we have collected data.

Inferential statistics allow us to infer statistical findings based on the sample to the whole population. For example, if researchers, using the Gen- eral Social Survey, a sample of the entire United States, find that attitudes toward homosexuality have been liberalizing since the 1970s, researchers *can infer* or predict that attitudes toward homosexuality have been liberal- izing in all of America since the 1970s.

In order to use inferential statistics, we need to make sure we have col- lected a probability sample. A probability sample uses chance and chance alone to determine who from the population will be chosen for the sample (see Part 3). All population members will have a known, positive probabil- ity of selection. It must also be a rather high-quality sample with a response rate of at least 70%. This way, we know it still represents the population and will provide us with unbiased point estimators. Bias is systematic error in the estimators.

With univariate statistics, we are interested in determining if our point estimates accurately reflect the central tendency in the population. The point estimator, mean or proportion in a category, is calculated from a sample and used to predict the population mean or proportion. The standard deviation of the mean is also a point estimator and can be used to predict the level of deviation about the mean in the population.

More questions? See questions 22, 31, and 79.

How Do We Infer the Population Parameter?

A major problem with using our sample point estimates to predict the population parameter (point estimate at population level) is that each single sample we choose, out of the infinite possible samples, could provide us with a somewhat different point estimate because the members of each sample will differ. Therefore, there is some uncertainty about how well the one chosen sample's estimate reflects the population parameter. Inferential statistics are designed to help us with these uncertainties.

One option is to create a range of possible population parameters. We learned in Q76 that 95% of the sample members of a bell curve are within two standard deviations of the mean. This mean only 5% falls outside that area. We can use that information to create a 95% range of population parameters called a confidence interval (CI). We calculate a 95% CI as the sample mean plus and minus the standard deviation multiplied by 1.96, which represents two standard deviations: $CI = \bar{X} \pm 1.96 * SE_{\bar{x}}$. In Q76, we had a bell curve distribution of GPA with a mean of 2.98 and standard deviation of .42. The lower boundary of the CI is 2.98 − (1.96*.42) = 2.2, and the upper CI boundary is 2.98 + (1.96*.42) = 3.8 or CI = 2.2 − 3.8. We are 95% confident that the population parameter is within the CI or between the values of 2.2 and 3.8. There will always be a 5% chance the population parameter is outside the CI.

For categorical variables, we can use the proportion in the modal category as our point estimate and calculate a CI around it. If P is the proportion in the category, then 1−P is the proportion not in the category. We can use this to calculate the sample standard deviation about P as $SD_p = \sqrt{\dfrac{P(1-P)}{n}}$.

If the proportion of Catholics in a U.S. sample is 23%, then P = .23 and 1−P = .77. In a sample of 1,500, the SD_p = .011. Then we can calculate a 95% CI about P using the same formula: .23 ± 1.96 * (.011) = .208 − .252. The proportion of Catholics in the United States is between 20.8% and 25.2%. The CI will be wider if the sample size is small. As the sample size gets larger, the CI will narrow. Therefore, a larger sample will give us a more precise range about the sample point estimate.

More questions? See questions 77, 78, and 80.

What Is Significance Testing?

Sometimes we come to our analyses with certain hypotheses and we want to assess whether or not our hypothesis is correct. A hypothesis is a proposition about a population characteristic or association. Sample data are used to test the hypotheses. For example, we may have started a study of education hypothesizing that the mean GPA level is 3.5. We can use a significance test to assess the hypothesis by comparing the sample mean GPA to the hypothesized value.

The significance test starts with two hypotheses. The first is the research hypothesis that the researcher is making. The second is called the null hypothesis. The null hypothesis contradicts the research hypothesis. It suggests there is no effect. In this example of GPA (see Q75 and Q76), the null hypothesis would be that GPA does not equal 3.5. It is the null hypothesis that is directly tested.

Once the hypothesis is stated, data are collected to test the hypothesis. In the education example, we are comparing the sample mean GPA, which is 2.98 on a sample of 1,355, to the hypothesized population GPA of 3.5. The question now is this: *Is a sample value of 2.98 likely to be generated from a population that has an average GPA of 3.5?* The next step is to calculate a P-value to assess statistical significance. The P-value is the probability that the test statistic is the true value of the population. The smaller the P-value, the more strongly the data contradict the null hypothesis, and the more strongly we can reject that the sample finding was due to random chance. We tend to use a P-value of less than .05 to reject the null hypothesis. This is equivalent to a 95% confidence interval. Using sample information, as well as information generated from known characteristics of the normal curve distribution (from a statistics textbook), the P-value is estimated to be .0014. As this is less than .05, we reject the null hypothesis. It is possible that the population mean is 3.5. Language is important here. We do not accept the research hypothesis—we only reject or fail to reject the null hypothesis.

More questions? See questions 75, 78, and 79.

Assessing Associations With Bivariate Statistical Tests and Regression

What Is Meant by Association Between Variables?

I t is very important to understand each variable in the dataset. However, it is rare that univariate statistics can answer our research question. We are far more interested in whether or not there are associations between our variables and what those associations mean.

An association between two variables means they will vary together in a pattern. This means that as one variable goes up or down, an associated variable will either go up or down. If both variables go up together, then they have a positive association. For example, as years of education completed goes up, income also goes up. Education and income have a positive association. If one variable goes down and one goes up, the variables have an inverse or negative relationship. For example, as years of education completed goes up, body mass index (BMI) goes down. If one variable goes up or down and the other variable doesn't change at all, then there is no association.

When looking at pairs of variables, we are interested in (1) if is there an association, (2) the direction of the relationship, and (3) the magnitude or size of the association. We are also interested in determining if the association is statistically significant. That is, can we infer (use inferential statistics) that the association found in the sample also exists in the population? The larger the association, the easier it is to determine that an association is statistically significant. Lastly, we are generally interested in labeling one of the variables as the dependent variable and the other as the independent variable. The dependent variable is the one whose changes depend upon changes in the independent variable. Income levels depend upon education levels.

Assessing association, as can be seen in Table 81.1, differs depending upon the measurement of the dependent and independent variables. For example, if both variables are continuous, we can visually display the associations with a scatterplot and test if the association is significant using a Pearson's correlation coefficient. Ordinal variables can be treated like continuous variables if there are a large number of values and they are normally distributed. Otherwise, treat them like categorical variables. Questions 82 to 85 focus on these associations and their tests.

Table 81.1 Tests of Association by Variable Measurement

Dependent Variable	Independent Variable	Visual Display of Association	Statistical Test of Association	Question
Continuous	Continuous	Scatter plots	Pearson's correlation coefficient	82–83
Continuous	Categorical	Group means Bar charts	t-tests / ANOVA	84
Ordinal (five or more values)	Continuous	Scatter plots	Pearson's correlation coefficient	82–83
Ordinal (five or more values)	Categorical	Group means, Bar charts	t-tests / ANOVA	84
Categorical	Categorical	Chi-square table	Fisher's exact, chi-square	85
Ordinal (fewer than five categories)	Categorical	Chi-square table	Gamma	85

Graphical plots of association as well as numerical indicators of association can be estimated using any standard statistical software package including Microsoft Excel.

More questions? See questions 72, 78, and 80.

How Do We Assess an Association Between Two Continuous Variables?

I f both variables are continuous, we can graphically display the associa-tion using a scatter plot. From the scatter plot we can tell the direction of the association, the size of association from the slope, and whether or not the relationship is linear. We can measure size, direction, and statistical significance of the association using Pearson's correlation coefficient.

The correlation coefficient is a numerical index that ranges from −1 to +1. A correlation of 0 means no association. A correlation of −1 means a perfectly correlated inverse association. That is, as the independent variable increases by one unit the dependent variable decreases by one unit. Lastly a correlation of +1 means a perfect positive association. In other words, as the independent variable increases by one unit, so does the dependent variable.

Table 82.1 presents common interpretations of the correlation coef-ficient. The closer the correlation coefficient is to 0, the smaller the size of the association, and the closer the correlation coefficient is to +1 or −1, the stronger the association. Therefore, a correlation of .65 or a correlation of −.65 would both be described as a moderate correlation.

Table 82.1 Value of Correlation Coefficient		
Positive	Negative	Interpret as
0 – .2	0 – –2	No association
>.2 – .4	<–2 – –4	Small association
>.4 – .6	<–4 – –6	Moderate association
>.6 – .8	<–6 – –8	Strong association
>.8 – 1.0	<–8 – –10	Very strong association

More questions? See questions 81, 83, and 86.

83

How Do We Determine if a Correlation Between Two Continuous Variables Is Statistically Significant?

I f a correlation exists in the sample, is it due to chance? What is the likelihood that the correlation exists in the original population? This is inferential statistics (see Q80) on a bivariate analysis. The null hypothesis is that there is no correlation, and the alternative research hypothesis is that there is an association between the two continuous variables. We assess statistical association again, by comparing our findings to a test statistic that comes from the appropriate underlying distribution. In this case, it would be the normal bell curve distribution. If the association is significant, the P-value will be less than .05, in which case we reject the null hypothesis. If, however, the P-value is greater than .05, we fail to reject the null hypothesis. Any statistical package can calculate a correlation and statistical significance.

Figures 83.1a and b present a scatterplot and correlation table of education and income. The plot shows a linear association with a positive relationship. The correlation coefficient is .455, which is a moderate, positive association. The correlation is statistically significant, as the P-value of .000 (sig in table) is greater than the cut-off of .05 (see Q80).

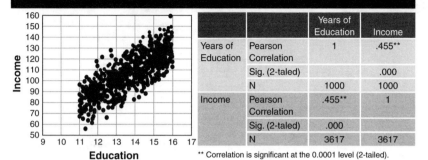

Figures 83.1a and b   Scatter Plot and Correlation Table of Education and Income

		Years of Education	Income
Years of Education	Pearson Correlation	1	.455**
	Sig. (2-taled)		.000
	N	1000	1000
Income	Pearson Correlation	.455**	1
	Sig. (2-taled)	.000	
	N	3617	3617

** Correlation is significant at the 0.0001 level (2-tailed).

Source: Americans Changing Lives, Wave 1, 1986

More questions? See questions 81, 82, and 84.

How Do We Assess Association Between a Categorical and a Continuous Variable?

G rouping variables are categorical, and we often want to know if the mean of some continuous variable differs by group membership. For example, does education vary by gender? If the categorical variable has two values, then we can use a statistical technique called an independent samples t-test. A t-test assesses the null hypothesis that the mean is equal across both groups. The alternative hypothesis is that they are not equal. The larger the difference between the groups, the more likely it is to be statistically significant.

Table 84.1 presents the results of a t-test on years of education grouped by gender. The difference in mean educational level is very small at .11, and the P-value is greater than .05; therefore, we fail to reject the null hypothesis and conclude there is no gender difference in mean educational levels.

If the categorical variable has more than two categories, we can use an analysis of variance technique called ANOVA. The null hypothesis again is that there are no differences in the means across the groups, while the alternative hypothesis is that at least one group is statistically different. The test statistic here is the F rather than a t, but essentially it does the same thing. The ANOVA in most statistical packages will only test the difference but not provide the means or the mean group differences. To get the means to make the table, we will have to run the means separately for each group in addition to the ANOVA. Table 84.2 presents the results of an ANOVA comparing racial group differences in education. In this case, one racial group mean education level is significantly different from the rest, and we reject the null.

Table 84.1	*T*-Test for Gender Differences in Educational Attainment					
	N	Mean Education	Standard Deviation	Mean Difference	t	P-value
Women	506	13.63	1.40	.11	.640	.522
Men	494	13.52	1.46			

	N	Mean Education	Standard Deviation	Mean Diff with Black	ANOVA F	P-value
White	2323	12.04	3.11	−1.65		
Black	1174	10.39	3.74		94.17	<.0001
Other	120	10.89	4.69	−.50		

Table 84.2 ANOVA Test for Racial Differences in Educational Attainment

Source: Americans Changing Lives Data, Wave 1, from Inter-university Consortium for Political and Social Research, University of Michigan, 2012.

More questions? See questions 81, 85, and 90.

How Do We Assess Association Between Two Categorical Variables?

Working with categorical variables can be a little challenging because the numbers assigned to each category are meaningless. To assess the association, we run a procedure called a cross-tabulation or crosstabs. Table 85.1 provides a crosstabs between race and wealth with wealth measured dichotomously as having assets worth less than $10K or $10K or more. The first number in each box is a count of all the respondents that fit in the two categories that bisect that box or cell. For example, there are 1,096 whites with less than $10K in assets. The second number in each box is the column percentage.

To determine if there is an association, we look at the percentages rather than counts, as percentages are comparable. If the percentage in each column is the same for each racial group, then there is no association. This reflects the null hypothesis of no association (independence). If the percentage in each column is different for at least one of the racial groups, then there could be a statistically significant difference (dependence). This is the alternate hypothesis. The hypotheses are tested with a chi-square test. For Table 85.1, the chi-square is 271.18 and its P-value is <.0001. Therefore, we reject the null hypothesis of no association. We would interpret this as whites are twice as likely to have $10K or more in assets compared to blacks and other racial groups.

	Less than $10K in Assets	$10K in Assets or More	Total
Table 85.1	**Crosstab of Having $10K or More in Assets by Race**		
White	1,096 47%	1,227 52%	2323 100%
Black	888 75%	286 24%	1174 100%
Other	88 73%	32 26%	120
Total	2,072	1,545	3,616

Source: Americans Changing Lives, Wave 1, 2012.

More questions? See questions 74, 81, and 84.

How Do We Display and Report These Bivariate Statistics?

There are two important pieces of information that need to be presented from bivariate analyses: (1) some form of point estimate for the association, and (2) the P-value that lets us know the association is significant. What exactly is displayed will depend upon the bivariate association procedure used.

If we are presenting a correlation, then we do not need to display the entire correlation table that a statistical package provides to us. We can simply state the size of the correlation. For example, in Q83 we correlated education and income. We can say "Education and income are moderately and positively correlated at .455, and the association is statistically significant at P <.0001."

If presenting on means from group difference tests, we can use a table to present the point estimates. In this case, the point estimates would be the means and mean differences. Alternatively, we can present the means in a bar chart to compare the means visually. Once again, we would include the P-value as part of the information. For example, in Q84, we assessed racial differences in education. A bar chart with mean years of educational attainment will provide the needed point estimates. We would say "Whites, on average, have attained about 2 years more of education compared to blacks and other racial groups, and this difference is statistical significant at P-value = .0001."

For crosstabs, we can present either the entire crosstab table or bar charts of the percentages in each category along with the P-value associated with the chi-square test. We would interpret the percentages as 52% of whites have $10k or more in assets compared to blacks and other races, who have 24% and 26%, respectively (see Q85).

More questions? See questions 83, 84, and 85.

What Is Linear Regression, and What Are Its Benefits?

Linear regression is a common statistical technique for assessing association. Regression allows us to (1) assess if there is a linear relationship between the variables, (2) assess the size of the relationship, (3) see if the relationship remains after including additional variables in the regression model, and (4) statistically test if the relationship can be generalized to the population from which it was drawn.

The first step is to determine which variable is the dependent variable. In the research question that started the survey project, the thing we most wanted to explain was our dependent variable. That is the variable we will be regressing on one or more independent variables. The independent variables are those variables that we think will be associated with and explain the response outcomes (variation) in the dependent variable.

Once we know which variable is the dependent variable, we need to know how it is measured. If it is continuous, then we can use ordinary least squares regression (OLS). If it is dichotomous, we will use logistic regression. If it is ordinal or categorical with more than two categories, we will use ordered logit or multinomial logit regressions. For this book, there is only room to focus on OLS regression. Please seek out a statistics textbook for more help.

Regression allows us to use more than two independent variables. This is its most important benefit. It allows us to determine the unbiased relationship between two variables by controlling for the effects of other variables. In Q82, we looked at a correlation between education and income. If we know, however, that women tend to attain higher education and receive lower income, then the correlation coefficient may be biased (have error) due to what is called a *confound*. A confound happens when a third variable is associated with both the dependent and independent variables but is not accounted for in the statistical analysis. We can regress income simultaneously, however, on both education and gender to get unbiased results.

More questions? See questions 71, 72, and 78.

What Is OLS Regression With a Continuous Independent Variable?

O LS regression takes the form of an equation: $Y_i = a + b_1 X_{1i}$ + error, where Y_i is the dependent variable, X_1 is the independent variable, "i" is for each person in the sample, "a" and "b_1" are estimated regression coefficients, and the error is the difference between the original observed "Y" variable and the regression equation predicted "Y" value. It includes everyone associated with the dependent variable that was not directly included in the regression equation. In the above equation, we have included only one independent or predictor variable. The intercept is represented by "a" in the equation and is the value of Y when the X independent variable = 0. The regression coefficient "B_1" measures the association between X and Y. B_1 is often called the slope.

We will look at the association between income and education as we did for Q82. The equation is Income = $a + b_1$Education$_1$ + error. We can run this regression in any standard statistical software package. The results are shown in Table 88.1. The parameter estimates are the "a" and "b_1". We can rewrite the regression equation replacing the "a" with the intercept, –9662.92, and the "b_1" with 2878.61: Y = –9662.92 + (2878.61)*Education. Now that the equation is estimated, we leave off the error term. We can interpret the regression. The intercept can be interpreted as follows: "For those with zero years of education, the average income earned is estimated to be \$–9,662.92." There are very few people, if any, with zero years of education, and so, often, the intercept is extrapolated and might not make sense. The association between education and income is found in the b_1 parameter, which can be interpreted as, "an increase in education by one year is associated with a \$2,878.61 higher level of income on average."

Table 88.1 Regressing Income on Education ($n = 3,617$)				
	Parameter Estimate	Standard Error	*T* Value	*P*-Value
Intercept (a)	−9662.92	1123.37	−8.60	<.0001
Education (b₁)	2878.61	93.74	30.71	<.0001

Source: Americans Changing Lives, Wave 1, 2012.

More questions? See questions 83, 87, and 89.

QUESTION 89

How Do We Know if the Regression Coefficients Are Statistically Significant?

In the previous question we regressed income on education. We are interested in the relationship between education and income. That relationship is called the slope. We want to know if the relationship between education and income is statistically significant in the population. We set the null hypothesis to say there is no association between education and income or $b_1 = 0$. The alternative hypothesis is that $b_1 \neq 0$. The regression results tell us that the b_1 slope is 2,878.61, but how do we know if it is statistically significant?

In Q88 we looked only at the parameter estimates to use in the regression equation. But there are several additional items in the table. Table 89.1 presents that same table of regression results. The standard error column gives us measures of dispersion about the sample intercept and sample slope for education and income. The "t" value is calculated by dividing the parameter estimate by the standard error. We compare the calculated "t" value to the comparable t-test statistic that is based on the normal distribution to determine if the slope is statistically significant. If the "t" value is greater than the t-test statistic, the P-value will be less than .05. The statistical package used will make this comparison and provide the P-value for us. Table 89.1 shows that the slope parameter estimate has a P-value of <.0001; therefore, we reject the null hypothesis of no association. The slope is statistically significant.

Table 89.1	Regressing Income on Education (n = 3,617)			
	Parameter Estimate	Standard Error	t-Value	P-Value
Intercept (a)	−9662.92	1123.37	−8.60	<.0001
Education (b_1)	2878.61	93.74	30.71	<.0001

Source: Americans Changing Lives, Wave 1, 2012.

More questions? See questions 78, 83, and 88.

90

How Do We Interpret OLS Regression With a Categorical Independent Variable?

I n Q84, we examined group differences in a continuous dependent variable using a t-test or an ANOVA. Regression provides similar results with a single categorical independent variable. If we regress income on gender, the equation is Income = a + b_1*male. The variable "male" is a dummy variable created from the dichotomous gender variable. Male = 0 for all the females, and male = 1 for all the males. Recall that the intercept is the value of Y, or income in this case, when the X variable (gender) equals 0. Well, when male = 0, we have all the females. Therefore, in a regression with a dummy variable, we can interpret the intercept as the average outcome (income) for the zero category (females). Table 90.1 presents the regression results of income regressed on gender. We can interpret the intercept as "On average, women earn $20,573." We can interpret the slope for male as a deviation from the intercept "On average, men earn $7,399.86 more than women." This difference is statistically significant at P = <.0001.

What if the categorical variable has more than two categories? We will make k-1 (k = # of categories) dummy variables to include in the regression equation. If the categorical variable has three categories, like the race variable with white, black, and other, we will make k-1 or 2 dummy variables to include in the regression equation. If we include dummy variables for black and other race, the regression equation is

Table 90.1	Income Regressed on Gender (n = 3,617)			
	Parameter Estimate	Standard Error	tValue	P-Value
Intercept (a)	20,573	456.42	45.08	<.0001
Male (b_1)	7399.86	744.89	9.93	<.0001

Source: Americans Changing Lives, Wave 1, 2012.

Income = a + b1*black + b2*other race. In this equation, white is the left out category and exists as the intercept when black = 0 and other race = 0. Table 90.2 presents the regression results. Again, we interpret the intercept for the missing category (reference category) of white as "Whites earned an average income of $27,030." The estimates for blacks and other races are deviations from the intercept. Blacks on average earned $10,739 less income compared to whites, and other racial groups earned $5,800 less than whites, on average.

Table 90.2   Income Regressed on Race ($n = 3,617$)

	Parameter Estimate	Standard Error	t Value	P-Value
Intercept (a)	27,030	444.28	60.84	<.0001
Black (b₁)	–10,739	766.79	–14.01	<.0001
Other Race (b₂)	–5,800.54	2004.62	–2.89	.0038

Source: Americans Changing Lives, Wave 1, 2012.

More questions? See questions 84, 88, and 89.

How Do We Interpret Linear Regression With More Than One Predictor Variable?

A great strength of regression is that it allows us to include multiple independent variables in the regression equation. We can regress income on both education and gender simultaneously. The equation is Income = $a + b_1*$education $+ b_2*$male. We would want to do this because gender is related to both income and education. Therefore, the parameter estimate for the regression of income on education alone is too big; it is confounded with gender. Figure 91.1 shows what this means. If we regress income on education only, the parameter estimate will be too large because it will include areas "a" and "b". Area "b" indicates an area of overlap between gender, education, and income. If we include gender in the regression model, we can isolate the independent effect of education on income. The independent effect of education on income, when controlling for gender, is called the partial regression coefficient. Table 91.1 shows the multiple regression results.

The intercept is the value of income when education equals 0 and male = 0. It can be interpreted as the average income for females with no education, which is –$11,502. The parameter estimate for education is slightly smaller than it was in the bivariate regression in Q88. It can be

Figure 91.1 Venn Diagram of Income, Education, and Gender

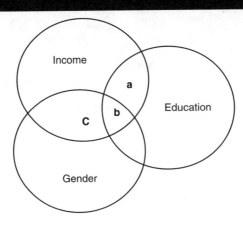

interpreted as an additional year of education is associated with a $2,731 higher income on average and controlling for gender. The parameter estimate for male is also smaller than it was in the bivariate regression shown in Q90. It can be interpreted as a deviation from the intercept. On average, men earn $6,324 more compared to women, controlling for education. Both education and male are statistically significant effects.

	Parameter Estimate	Standard Error	t Value	P-Value
Table 91.1 Regressing Income on Education and Gender (n = 3,617)				
Intercept (a)	−11,502	1126.45	−10.21	<.0001
Education (b$_1$)	2,831.90	92.74	30.54	<.0001
Male (b$_2$)	6,323.92	665.14	9.51	.0038

Source: Americans Changing Lives, Wave 1, 2012.

More questions? See questions 87, 88, and 90.

How Do We Display and Report These Regression Statistics?

A s mentioned in Q86, there are two important pieces of information: (1) a point estimate of the association between two variables is important for letting the audience know the magnitude and direction of the association, and (2) the P-value lets the audience know if the association is statistically significant in the population from which the sample was drawn.

In regression analyses, the parameter estimates along with their standard errors are often displayed in a table, much like they are in the tables found in Q90 and Q91.

A graphical display can also illuminate the relationships between the variables. Figure 92.1 presents a graph of the associations found in Table 91.1. We can take the results from the table and put them into the regression equation like this: Income = −11,502 +2831.90*education + 6,323.92*male. To graph this equation, we simply solve for females at each education level and solve for males at each education level and then graph those two lines across education on the x axis and income on the

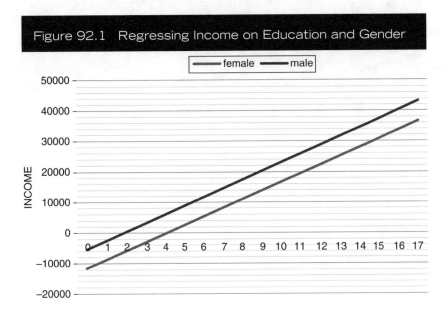

Figure 92.1 Regressing Income on Education and Gender

y axis. In Figure 92.1, we can see that at every year of education, men earn $6,323.92 more than women. Income increases for both men and women with each additional year of education attained.

More questions? See questions 86, 90, and 91.

Writing Up the Analyses in Report Form

93

Who Is My Audience, and Why Does It Matter?

Conducting a survey to answer a research question is a lot of work. As researchers, we want to make sure all that work is fruitful and that our audience can understand the findings and act upon them accordingly. Therefore, we write up a report to present our findings targeting a specific audience. If this is an academic endeavor with an academic audience, we will want to publish in an academic journal. Consequently, the write-up will be highly theoretical, and the audience will have a strong statistical knowledge. The methods used to both collect the data and analyze it must be presented in detail. Very sophisticated analyses can be presented as the results, and we can assume the audience can interpret the results easily. The presentation of the results will consist primarily of tables of statistical output possibly with one or more graphs.

If, however, the audience is a nonprofit organization that needed a program evaluation, or a for-profit client, we may want to replace the theoretical components and sophisticated analyses with more applied content and descriptive analyses. Applied content is more user friendly and has less jargon. For example, if a nonprofit program is being evaluated, the report will contain a simple description of how the evaluation was implemented and evaluated. It is written broadly with a focus on clear and simple language. In addition, more graphical displays of the analyses may be easier for this audience to consume. In the report, only include enough methods of the survey research to assist in the understanding of the report. Include the bulk of the methods to an appendix at the end of the report. This way, those that want to read the methods still can. Finally, create an executive summary. An executive summary takes up one full page. It is a shortened version of the full report including a summary of the most important findings, and it includes several recommendations for the client or nonprofit.

More questions? See questions 94, 95, and 100.

What Is a Good Report Outline?

There are several good report outlines that can be used. In Table 94.1, outlines are presented for an academic journal, an evaluation report, and a policy-type report. All three have a lot in common. The abstract for a journal article is not the same as an executive summary. Abstracts tend to be around 150 words, whereas executive summaries are one full page. Journals supplement the abstract with an introduction. Evaluation reports skip directly to the background piece. In a journal article, the background is a review of existing research on the topic of interest. For evaluations, it

Table 94.1   Outlines of Three Types of Reports

Journal Article	Evaluation Report	Policy Report
Title page	Title page	Title page
Abstract	Executive Summary	Policy Memo/Executive Summary
Introduction		Introduction—describe the policy problem
Background/ literature review	Background—Origin of program, program aims, participants, staff involved	Background—describe alternative solutions
Methods	Description of the evaluation	Analysis
Results	Results	Results
Discussion	Discussion	
	Costs and Benefits	
Conclusion	Conclusion	Recommendations
References	References	References
Appendices		

consists of describing the program including its aims, participants, and staff. A policy report uses the introduction for describing the problem that needs policy attention. A policy report uses the background information to describe alternative solutions or practices or what might happen with no action. The methods discuss how data were collected and analyzed for each report. The results section presents the findings from the analyses. Discussion, costs and benefits, recommendations, and conclusions are all about how to integrate the findings into recommending solutions.

More questions? See questions 93, 95, and 100.

How Much of the Methodology Needs to Be Included in the Report?

The purpose of the methodology is to clearly and transparently demonstrate how the data were collected and analyzed. That means all of the methodology needs to be included. Start by discussing the data-collection process. What sampling methods were used, and what is the final response rate? Were any cases dropped, and for what reasons? The definitions of the constructs and the survey questions used to measure them should be included along with any data manipulations that were done to them during the analysis phase. In the data-cleaning process, were there any outliers, and how were they handled? What other issues came up, and what were the decisions made to address them? Lastly, discuss the analysis techniques used and why.

Another purpose of clearly and transparently describing the research methods is to allow the audience to evaluate the quality of the research and interpret the findings in light of that quality. Finally, clarity and transparency can ensure that the research was conducted ethically, independent of some hidden agenda.

Good methodological description does not always have to be included in the body of the report. For academic audiences, replication is extremely important, so having very detailed methods in the body of the report or journal article is necessary in order for someone to replicate the research. For lay or professional audiences, a good but brief summary in the body of the report should be sufficient as long as all the details of the methodology are included in an appendix to the report. This way the audience will not be distracted by a long technical piece. This will allow those members of your lay or professional audience who understand methods to be able to read them in the appendix and evaluate the report with that knowledge.

More questions? See questions 93, 94, and 100.

What Are the Most Important Parts of the Analyses to Include in the Report?

Before starting to write up an analysis-based report, most researchers will spend a good amount of time understanding exactly what the story is that the data are showing us. Once we have a good handle on the story, we will present only those parts of the analysis that help to tell that story. So, the first cut is to eliminate any interesting results that may distract from the main story. To be clear, "distraction" does not mean that it hurts the story we want to tell; rather, it means an interesting rabbit hole that does not pertain to the main story of the findings. Anything related to the story we want to tell, whether it is positive or negative, must be presented. Stick closely to the main findings of the story.

Once we have limited our findings to a primary story, we want to present our statistical parameters, whether they are the simple measures of central tendency discussed in Part 8 or the regression coefficients discussed in Part 9. When starting to present the findings, we often start with a table of descriptive statistics that provide the audience with a good idea of who is in the sample. Measures of central tendency and variation are appropriate for this purpose.

For bivariate analyses with categorical data, a crosstab or a bar chart might be the best way to present the results. These can show modal categories across both variables. For continuous variables, a table of correlations or scatter plots might be appropriate to present the relationships. For associations between continuous and categorical variables, tables or line graphs will work to present the findings.

When shifting from descriptive analyses to inferential statistics, we need to include three things: the main statistical coefficient, a measure of variation (standard error from the regression output), and some level of statistical significance. Typically P-values are presented. It is normative to use a P-value of less than .05 ($p = <.05$) to determine if a finding is statistically significant at the 95% confidence level.

More questions? See questions 81, 92, and 98.

97

How Do We Report on the Sample of Respondents?

B efore getting to the results of the study, it is important to let your audience know who is in the sample that is being analyzed. This helps the audience get a feel for the context of the analyses. Who is included in the sample? What is their average age, gender, race, religion, education, and income? Where do they live? Is there something special about this group? If you are evaluating a program, it will be important to include length of time in the program, how many started but left the program prior to completing it, and how many completed it.

Box 97.1 Example Table and Descriptive Write-Up of the Table

Table 10.1 Descriptive Statistics of the Sample (averages and [standard deviations] or percentages)

	Men	Women
Age	51 (2.4)	53 (3.1)
Educational attainment (years)	11.6 (2.6)	13.2 (1.7)
% Earning more than $100k	22%	9.6%
Sample Size	500	510

The sample is shown in Table 10.1. There were 500 men and 510 women in the sample. The average age is 51 for men and 53 for women. Women have attained approximately two more years of education than men at 13.2 years. Twenty-two percent of men earned over $100,000 dollars compared to just 9.6 percent of the women.

A table that includes basic univariate descriptive statistics (see Part 8 for help with univariate descriptive statistics) will help the audience get a feel for the sample. It will also give the report writer something to describe. Box 97.1 provides an example of a table with write-up.

A table always helps the writer to organize the write-up of the sample description. If there are a couple of really important aspects about the sample that we want to highlight, then we can make them special by including a graph about them, such as a bar chart or pie chart. The graphs will provide emphasis to that which is important, so do not overwhelm the audience with too many graphs.

More questions? See questions 95, 96, and 98.

QUESTION

98

How Many Charts and Tables Should We Include in the Report?

The number of charts and tables that should be included depends upon who the audience is, as well as the purpose of the report. For an academic audience, most journals limit the number of tables and charts to five or fewer. Therefore, we often see only a few, but really large tables in academic journals. One of those tables will be an introduction to the sample used for the analyses.

For lay audiences, these really long tables may be overwhelming and hard to understand. Important information may get lost. Therefore, for a lay audience, create an outline of the findings section, and for each set of findings, include at least one table and chart. The table that describes the sample can be split up into several tables if that improves understanding. The table can summarize all the findings, and the chart can highlight the most important finding that we want the audience to understand from this section. It is possible that we may want more than one chart in a section if there are multiple important take-away points. For example, if there are five sections of questions on the survey, it makes sense to have five separate sections in the results section of the report—one for each survey section. Later in the findings, when bivariate analyses or regressions are presented, these can be additional sections. Therefore, with a lay audience and a report, use as many tables and charts as is necessary to tell the full story.

However, too many tables and charts might be a distraction from the central points of the report. Therefore, edit the report after it is written, but before it is sent to the client, employer, or lay audience, to ensure that none of the findings sections are confusing, overwhelming, or a distraction from the main points.

More questions? See questions 95, 96, and 97.

How Do We Describe Charts and Tables in the Report?

If a picture is worth a thousand words, a table or chart must be worth at least 500 words. If that is the case, why can't the table or chart stand alone? Why must it be described in words as well? Charts and tables, like pictures, contain many messages and they can stand alone. But pictures are art, and the artists want each member of the audience to walk away with their own interpretation of the picture—their own individual understanding of it. If working within a particular discipline, check the style guidelines on producing charts and figures (e.g., APA).

Tables and charts might feel like art given all the time spent to produce them, but they are not art. They are designed with a specific message in mind, and we write up the tables and charts in the text of the reports to ensure the audience is getting the correct message—the message the research findings are providing. Some audience members may have a particular agenda or perspective, and that is what they will look for in the charts and tables. The report is generally designed to be persuasive—to persuade the audience that a program was successful or there are needed policy changes. Without a clear written message alongside the tables and charts, the various members of the audience will come up with their own individual interpretation, their own agenda, and the effectiveness of the report will be lost.

Therefore, the text write-up does not need to describe everything in the table. The write-up needs to highlight the important findings and explain to the audience how to interpret those findings. This is what will persuade the audience. The text can acknowledge that there are other findings that are not being written up because they are not pertinent at this moment or to the research question, or that there is no way to address these other findings, and therefore they are irrelevant for a policy report. Or authors can simply decide to ignore superfluous findings.

More questions? See questions 93, 98, and 100.

100

What Is an Executive Summary, and Why Is It Important?

An executive summary is a one-page summary of the entire report. The audience should be able to read only the executive summary and know exactly the information contained in the more detailed report. For that reason, it should be the last part written. In fact, it should be written in the same format as the report. It will include a statement of the problem and any background information, describe the study, present important research findings, and make recommendations based on those findings. It should have short, concise paragraphs, in order to fit on one page.

Executive summaries are important communication tools. This is the first thing the decision makers or policy makers or funders will read about the project. The decisions, policies, and even potential future funding will depend greatly on the quality and professionalism of the summary and its attached report. Therefore, authors need to use the evidence from the findings to persuade the audience of the importance or relevance of the research findings and the prevalence and importance of the problem it addresses.

Because executive summaries are short and concise, it is easy to see that the arguments made in the executive summary may be more superficial compared to the arguments in the full report. For a good executive summary, however, that will harm its ability to be persuasive. Therefore, more time and attention needs to be spent in writing up the summary so that it does not become a watered-down version of the final report. It needs to be the opposite of a watered-down version. It needs to have strong, tight arguments. A successful executive summary is one in which the authors have spent a great deal of time and energy focusing on creating a concise synthesis of the entire report.

More questions? See questions 93, 94, and 99.

References and Resources

Part 1: Understanding What Surveys Are and How They Are Used

Dillman, D. A., Smyth, J. D., & Christian, L. M. (2009). *Internet, mail, and mixed-mode surveys: The tailored design method* (3rd ed.). Hoboken, NJ: Wiley.

Ruel, E., Wagner, W. E., & Gillespie, B. J. (2016). *The practice of survey research.* Thousand Oaks, CA: Sage.

Part 2: Addressing Ethical Concerns in Survey Research

National Commission for the Protection of Human Subjects of Biomedical and Behavioral Research. (1979). *Belmont Report.* Washington, DC: US Department of Health and Human Services.

Part 3: Selecting a Sample

Cohen, J. (1992). Statistical power analysis. *Current Directions in Psychological Science, 1*(3), 98–101.

Kalton, G. (1983). *Introduction to survey sampling.* Newbury Park, CA: Sage.

Kish, L. (1995). *Survey sampling.* New York, NY: Wiley.

Lenth, R. V. (2001). Some practical guidelines for effective sample size determination. *The American Statistician, 55*(3), 187–193.

Part 4: Writing Good Survey Questions

Bradburn, N., Sudman, S., & Wansink, B. (2004). *Asking questions* (2nd ed.). San Francisco, CA: Jossey-Bass.

Converse, J. M., & Presser, S. (1986). *Survey questions: Handcrafting the standardized questionnaire.* Thousand Oaks, CA: Sage.

Inter-University Consortium for Political and Social Research. (2009). *Guide to social science data preparation and archiving: Best practices throughout the data life cycle* (4th ed.). Ann Arbor, MI: Author.

Krumpal, I. (2013). Determinants of social desirability bias in sensitive surveys: A literature review. *Quality and Quantity, 47*(4), 2025–2047.

Lenth, R. V. (2001). Some practical guidelines for effective sample size determination. *The American Statistician, 55*(3), 187–193.

Part 5: Establishing the Reliability and Validity of Survey Questions

Carmines, E. G., & Zeller, R. A. (1979). *Reliability and validity assessment.* Beverly Hills, CA: Sage.

Cronbach, L. J. (1951). Coefficient alpha and the internal structure of tests. *Psychometrika, 16,* 297–334.

DeMaio, T. J., Rothgeb, J., & Hess, J. (1998). Improving survey quality through pretesting. *Proceedings of the Section on Survey Research Methods, American Statistical Association* (vol. 3), 50–88.

DeVellis, R. F. (2011). *Scale development theory and applications.* Newbury Park, CA: Sage.

Presser, S., Couper, M. P., Lessler, J. T., Martin, E., Martin, J., Rothgeb, J., & Singer, E. (2007). Methods for testing and evaluating survey questions. In S. Presser, J. M. Rothgeb, M. P. Couper, J. T. Lessler,

E. Martin, J. Martin, & E. Singer (Eds.), *Methods for testing and evaluating survey questionnaires* (1–22). San Francisco, CA: Wiley.

Part 6: Conducting the Survey

de Leeuw, E., Callegaro, M., Hox, J., Korendijk, E., & Lensvelt-Mulders, G. (2007). The influence of advance letters on response in telephone surveys: A meta-analysis. *Public Opinion Quarterly, 71*(3), 413–443.

Olson, K. (2006). Survey participation, nonresponse bias, measurement error bias, and total bias. *Public Opinion Quarterly, 70*(5), 737–758.

Part 7: Entering and Cleaning the Data

Ruel, E., Wagner, W. E., & Gillespie, B. J. (2016). *The practice of survey research.* Thousand Oaks, CA: Sage.

Part 8: Exploring the Data With Univariate Statistical Analysis

Agresti, A., & Finlay, B. (1997). *Statistical methods for the social sciences* (3rd ed.). Upper Saddle River, NJ: Prentice Hall.

Wagner, W. E. (2014). *Using IBM SPSS statistics for research methods and social science statistics* (5th ed.). Thousand Oaks, CA: Sage.

Warner, R. M. (2009). *Applied statistics: From bivariate through multivariate techniques.* Thousand Oaks, CA: Sage.

Part 9: Assessing Associations With Bivariate Statistical Tests and Regression

Agresti, A., & Finlay, B. (1997). *Statistical methods for the social sciences* (3rd ed.). Upper Saddle River, NJ: Prentice Hall.

Wagner, W. E. (2014). *Using IBM SPSS statistics for research methods and social science statistics* (5th ed.). Thousand Oaks, CA: Sage.

Warner, R. M. (2009). *Applied statistics: From bivariate through multivariate techniques.* Thousand Oaks, CA: Sage.

Index

Mailed surveys, 69, 71
Mall surveyor, 42
Market research, 42
Mean, 97, 100, 103
    examining variation in continuous
        variables using the, 107–108
    sampling distribution of the, 29–30
Measurement error
    defined, 64
    minimizing, 59, 65
Measurement of level of survey
    questions, 54
Measurement reliability, 63
Measures of central tendency, 97,
    99–100, 141. See also Central
    tendency of the variable; Mean;
    Median
Measures of variation (dispersion), 97,
    99–100, 105, 141
Median, 97, 100, 103
    examining variation in continuous
        variables when using, 105–106
Medical research
    ethical concerns in, 13
    ethical oversight of, 15
Methodological documentation, ethics
    and, 14
Methodology, 17
Methods section, 138, 139, 140
Mode, 97
Multiple choice format, 53
Multivariable analyses, 97

National Research Act (1974), 15
National Survey of Families and
    Households (NSFH), 31
Negative set-up, avoiding in survey
    questions, 51
Nominal measurement, 54
Nominal variables, 54, 98
Nonprobability sampling, 24, 42
    convenience sample, 42
    judgment sample, 42
    quota sample, 42
    snowball sample, 42
Nonprofits, use of surveys, 4
Normal distribution, 103
"Not applicable" code, 86

NUDIST software, 94
Null hypothesis, 111, 118
Numeric variables, 90
NVivo software, 94

Open-ended questions, 53
    coding, 94
    data entry for, 87
    when to use, 55
Order of survey questions, 56
Ordinal measurement, 54, 99
Ordinal variables, 98, 100
    assessing association between, 115, 116
    estimating central tendency and
        variation in, 101–102
Ordinary least squares regression
    (OLS), 125
    with a categorical independent
        variable, 129–130
    with a continuous independent
        variable, 126–127
"Other, please specify" responses
    coding, 92–93
    data entry for, 87

Panel survey designs, 8–9
    conducting, 77
    confidentiality and, 19
    for evaluative research questions, 10
Parameter estimates, 133
Pearson's correlation coefficient, 115,
    116, 117
Pen and paper surveys, 69, 71
Pilot testing, 59, 66
Plotting distributions, 99
Point estimates, 100, 124, 133
Policy memo, 138
Policy report, outline for, 138–139
Population
    defining for research study, 23
    sampling from, 23
    using existing survey questions and
        relevance to researcher's, 50
Population mean, random sampling
    error and, 31, 32
Population parameter, inferring, 110
Postcard, announcing survey, 72
"Power" to detect an effect, 26